JAMES,
1 & 2 PETER

JAMES,
1 & 2 PETER

◆

H. A. IRONSIDE

Revised Edition

Introductory Notes by
John Phillips

LOIZEAUX
Neptune, New Jersey

First Edition 1947
Revised Edition 1996
© 1947, 1996 by Loizeaux Brothers

A Publication of Loizeaux Brothers, Inc.
A Nonprofit Organization, Devoted to the
Lord's Work and to the spread of His Truth

Unless otherwise indicated, Scripture quotations in this book
are from the King James version of the Bible.

Profile taken from *Exploring the Scriptures*
© 1965, 1970, 1989 by John Phillips

Library of Congress Cataloging-in-Publication Data

Ironside, H. A. (Henry Allan), 1876-1951.
James and 1 & 2 Peter / H. A. Ironside.—Rev. ed.
ISBN 0-87213-415-6 (pbk.: alk. paper)
1. Bible. N.T. James—Commentaries.
2. Bible. N.T. Peter—Commentaries.   I. Title.
BS2785.3.I76   1996
227'.9107—dc20   96-43742

Printed in the United States of America.
10 9 8 7 6 5 4 3 2 1

CONTENTS

JAMES

JAMES
BELIEF THAT BEHAVES

BY JOHN PHILLIPS

M any have debated the authorship of the book of James. The writer calls himself "James, a servant of God and of the Lord Jesus Christ." The traditional view is that he was "the Lord's brother" (Galatians 1:19), an individual prominent in the Jerusalem church and one who took a leading part in the Council of Jerusalem (Acts 15; see also Matthew 13:55; Galatians 2:9). During the Lord's earthly life James was not a believer, but the Lord appeared to him after His resurrection (1 Corinthians 15:7).

The Epistle is addressed to "the twelve tribes which are scattered abroad," but it is evident from its content that it is primarily addressed to Jewish Christians. It is generally agreed that the Epistle was written before the fall of Jerusalem and probably even before the Council of Jerusalem. Some maintain that it is the earliest of all the New Testament documents. It could well have been written to those who had been present in Jerusalem on the day of Pentecost and who had carried away with them the barest essentials of Christianity—in fact little more than the messiahship of Jesus. James wrote in the style of an Old Testament prophet. His language was vivid and picturesque. He covered a wide range of subjects and drew repeatedly on the Old Testament, even the Apocrypha. It has been pointed out that, more than any other book of the New Testament, the book of James reflects the language of the sermon on the mount. The book is quite evidently not intended to be a theological treatise but rather a moral appeal.

The book of James discusses the battles, the Bible, the brethren, the beliefs, the behavior, the boasting, and the burdens of the Christian.

I. INTRODUCTION (1:1)
II. THE CHRISTIAN AND HIS BATTLES (1:2-16)
    A. The Testings of Christians (1:2-12)
        1. The Purpose of Testings (1:2-11)
            a. Our Enlargement (1:2-4)
            b. Our Enlightenment (1:5-8)
            c. Our Ennoblement (1:9-11)
        2. The Profit of Testings (1:12)
    B. The Temptations of Christians (1:13-16)
        1. The Source of Temptations (1:13-14)
        2. The Course of Temptations (1:15-16)
III. THE CHRISTIAN AND HIS BIBLE (1:17-27)
    A. The Bible Likened to a Gift (1:17-18)
        1. It Brings Divine Light (1:17)
        2. It Brings Divine Life (1:18)
    B. The Bible Likened to a Graft (1:19-22)
        1. It Will Change the Fruit of Our Lips (1:19-20)
        2. It Will Change The Fruit of Our Lives (1:21-22)
    C. The Bible Likened to a Glass (1:23-27)
        1. In Which We Look to be Challenged (1:23-24)
        2. In Which We Look to be Changed (1:25-27)
IV. THE CHRISTIAN AND HIS BRETHREN (2:1-13)
    Partiality is a sin against:
    A. The Lord (2:1-7)
    B. The Law (2:8-13)
V. THE CHRISTIAN AND HIS BELIEFS (2:14-26)
    The truth that "faith without works is dead" is:
    A. Emphatically Declared (2:14-17)
    B. Energetically Debated (2:18-20)
    C. Eternally Decided (2:21-26)
VI. THE CHRISTIAN AND HIS BEHAVIOR (3:1–4:12)
    A. Sin in the Life Must Be Revealed (3:1–4:4)
        1. In the Mouth (3:1-12)

A Practical Book

The Epistle of James is highly practical, for James insisted throughout on a belief that behaves. Are testings and temptations being faced? Then the believer must see to it that he profits from the one and wins through to victory in the other. God may test but He does not tempt. The believer must distinguish between the two forms of experience. Is the believer reading his Bible? Then he must be sure to put its precepts into practice. Is there a temptation to show partiality to the rich and unkindness to the poor? That does not make much sense in the light of the way rich men usually behave. Does a man say he has faith? Then let him prove it by his works, as did Abraham and Rahab.

A Perfect Man

What is the test of a perfect man? The ability to hold his tongue, for of all the members it is the most unruly. Why do some Christians seem to get no answers to prayer? Either because they do not pray or because they have lustful motives when they do pray. How can a Christian make even the devil flee? Simply by submitting himself to God. What will be the reward of the grasping rich? In the last days the working class will rise and demand its rights. If a Christian is happy, how should he express his joy? In singing psalms. If a Christian is sick what should he do? Call for the elders of the church and get right with God.

A Personal Standard

Who can read an epistle like this without coming under conviction of personal failure and shortcoming? James has great skill in getting at the conscience and translating Christianity into the practical everyday living it is intended to be. This is a book by which we might well measure our lives.

Martin Luther's famous comment on James to the effect that it was "a veritable Epistle of straw" is based, of course, on the assumption that James contradicted Paul's doctrine of justification by faith alone. But that is not so. Actually, we are justified by faith in the sight of God and by works in the sight of man. The New Testament teaches that we are justified by grace, by blood, by faith, by works, and by God.

INTRODUCTION

Frederick W. Grant, the able and conscientious Bible expositor whose works have proved valuable to thousands of God's children, drew attention to the fact that in the New Testament we have an Epistle written by Jacob to the descendants of Israel. For our English name James is really the equivalent of Jacob (*Jacobos* in Greek), and is the same as *Jacques* in French, *Iago* in Italian, *Diego* in Spanish, and other forms in many different languages. But the meaning is ever the same, "the supplanter," the "heel-catcher" or "tripper-up." This is what Jacob of old was. "He took his brother by the heel in the womb" (Hosea 12:3), and he was ever crafty and tricky until renewed by divine grace when he became Israel, "a prince with God."

There were two called James among the twelve apostles who were selected by our Lord on earth: James the son of Zebedee, the brother of John the beloved disciple, and James the son of Alpheus, brother of Judas not Iscariot. Apparently neither of these wrote the Epistle we are to consider. Certainly James the son of Zebedee did not, for he was slain by Herod very soon after Pentecost. James the Less, as the other disciple is generally called, has been thought by some to be the writer of this letter. But the greater consensus of opinion credits it to another Jacob altogether—James the earthly half brother of our Lord. Many think of these two as identical, and there is a bare possibility that such may be the case. Writing on the Epistle of Jude many years ago, I expressed myself as fully persuaded of this, but further study has made me feel this position is probably wrong.

James the brother of Jesus occupied a prominent place in

13

the Jerusalem church, as mentioned in the book of Acts. He was considered by the early church as a son of Mary and Joseph, born after Jesus, who is called her first-born. In later years, when the idea of Mary's perpetual virginity began to be promulgated, it was suggested that James was a son of Joseph by a former marriage, and so only a stepbrother of our Lord. But the Scriptures appear to oppose this idea. See particularly Matthew 12:46-47; 13:55; Mark 3:31-32; Luke 8:19-20; and 1 Corinthians 9:5. All these passages would seem to prove conclusively that Mary had other children besides Jesus. We are told in John 7:5 that these brethren did not believe in the Messianic claims of Jesus during the time preceding His resurrection. But after He rose from the dead He appeared to James (1 Corinthians 15:7) and, undoubtedly as a result of this, he became a devoted follower of Him whom he had not understood before. It is evident from the record in the book of Acts that this man soon became an outstanding leader among the Christians in Jerusalem, so much so that some going from there to the churches founded by Paul are said to have come from James (Galatians 2:12), although he had already disavowed having authorized them to use his name as an endorsement of their legal teaching (Acts 15:24).

The fact that his name is mentioned first in Galatians 1:19 and 2:9: "James, Cephas, and John, who seemed to be pillars," is significant, and indicates the prominent place he held in the church at Jerusalem. We may dismiss, however, as mere unfounded tradition the story handed down from early days that he was consecrated by the apostles as the first bishop of Jerusalem. Nevertheless, he occupied the position of moderator at the council held to determine the attitude of that church toward the missionary work of Paul and Barnabas, as narrated in Acts 15. It was James who summed up the testimony given, and suggested the writing of a letter to assure Christians from among the nations that they were not considered as under obligation to observe Jewish customs.

That James himself was to the end intensely Jewish is evident from the advice he gave Paul when he came to Jerusalem bringing alms for his nation. James suggested that Paul should pay the expenses for some brethren who were about to complete their Nazarite vows, and Paul was preparing to do this as being made all things to all men so that he might win some, when he was arrested (Acts 21:17-33).

Many besides Martin Luther have thought that the teaching in the letter of James was contradictory to that of Paul as set forth in Romans and Galatians. But a careful examination of these letters will show that they were dealing with altogether different subjects. Paul wrote on justification before God; James on justification before men. Had Luther understood and taught this in his early days, he might have saved many of his followers from resting on mere credulity instead of knowing the reality of saving faith.

It is not possible to decide with any certainty just when the Epistle of James was written. Many have supposed it was the earliest New Testament book, designed to bridge the gulf between the old and new dispensations, and so to prepare the way for Paul's gospel, which was to follow. In so writing I do not mean to intimate that Paul preached a different gospel to that of the other apostles, for he vehemently denies this in Galatians 1:6-9. But the risen Lord gave to him a fuller understanding of the results of the work of Christ than had been revealed previously. He alone speaks of justification from all things, rather than mere forgiveness, precious as that is.

It is quite possible that James wrote very shortly after Pentecost. Yet his letter presupposes a reasonably full acquaintance with the great truths of Christianity and its diffusion throughout the entire world where the people of Israel were scattered. Because of this, others have concluded that instead of being the first inspired message to the twelve tribes in the new age, it may have been written quite late—after several of Paul's Epistles were in circulation, notably that to the Romans. In this case the teaching of justification by works in James 2 would be designed to correct a misunderstanding bordering on antinomianism on the part of some who were pushing Paul's teaching to an extreme he never intended.

The letter was addressed, not to any individual church or group of churches, as such, but to the twelve tribes of Israel in the dispersion—those twelve tribes of whom Paul speaks in his address before Agrippa (Acts 26:7). James wrote to these fellow Israelites putting before them the claims of Jesus the Lord of glory. The church and the synagogue were not yet fully separated from each other. Many believing Israelites mingled with their Jewish brethren in the synagogue services, where there was considerable liberty for those of diverse views to express themselves. But these considerations should not lead any Christian to ignore or look lightly upon this Epistle. After all, in the body of Christ all distinctions between Jew and Gentile are done away. And although there were Jewish groups of believers who did not fraternize fully with Gentile Christians, they were one in Christ whether they realized it or not. All moral and spiritual truth, wherever found, is for us who now believe in the Lord Jesus Christ and confirm Him as our Head.

The theme of the Epistle is a living faith—a faith that is evidenced by righteous living and godly behavior. Throughout the Epistle we will recognize a very close connection between its instruction and that given by our Lord in the sermon on the mount (Matthew 5–7). James deals not with deep and abstruse doctrinal themes but with practical Christian ethics.

CHAPTER ONE
A VICTORIOUS FAITH

It is a grave mistake to infer, as some have done, that this Epistle emphasizes works rather than faith. It stresses the importance of faith throughout, but shows that real faith is never separated from a life of piety.

The Salutation (James 1:1)

If we are correct in attributing the writing of this Epistle to James the Lord's brother, the manner in which he speaks of himself becomes all the more striking: "James, a servant of God and of the Lord Jesus Christ"! If he had known Christ as a brother in the flesh, he knew Him so no more. He honored Him as Lord and Messiah, and linked His name with that of God the Father. Whatever doubts James may have entertained concerning the claims of Jesus in the days of His flesh, he had none when writing his Epistle. All doubts had been dissipated by the resurrection of the One with whom he had sustained so intimate a relationship in the Nazareth home.

He wrote "to the twelve tribes which are scattered abroad." As a Jew himself, but a Jew who knew the Lord in the fullness of resurrection life, he wrote to all the Jewish brethren whose fathers had been for centuries dispersed among the nations, and who themselves were scattered far and wide. Many of these knew Jesus as the Christ. If any who did not have this knowledge would read this letter it was James's desire to bring them to know Jesus who is, in Himself, the fulfillment of all Israel's hopes.

It is not for those of us who are Gentile Christians to ignore this portion of Scripture as though it had no message for us. But just as the letters written by Paul to Gentile Christians were generally for all believers whatever their former nationality or relationship, so this Epistle contains precious and important truth for the edification and sanctification of all who, like its writer, are slaves of God and of Christ.

Patience in Adversity (James 1:2-4)

These verses in James 1 link very intimately with what Paul has written in Romans 5:1-5. It is no evidence of God's displeasure when His people are called on to pass through great trials. If one professes to have faith in the Lord he can be sure that his profession will be put to the test sooner or later. We so frequently lose courage and become despondent in the hour of temptation, instead of realizing that it is the very time when we should look up into the Father's face with confidence, knowing that He is working out some purpose in us which could not be worked out in any other way. We are called on to "count it all joy" when we fall into many trials. The word *temptation*, as used in the King James version, does not refer to our being tempted to sin, but rather to the testing of our faith, as when God tested Abraham.

Paul wrote that tribulation worketh patience, and James affirmed the same: "The trying of your faith worketh patience" (3). By nature we are inclined to be fretful and impatient. Even Christians sometimes rebel against the ways of God when these go contrary to their own desires. But he who learns to be submissive to whatever God permits glorifies Him who orders all things according to the counsel of His own will. David said his soul had quieted itself as a weaned child (Psalm 131:2). This is patience exemplified. When natural nourishment is suddenly taken from a baby and he is given other food more suitable for his age, he becomes peevish and fretful. But when he is gradually weaned all this is ended, and he accepts gratefully the food offered to him.

As we grow in this grace of patience until there is no longer any rebellion against the will of God, a strong Christian character is developed. We become mature and whole, no longer craving for what God sees fit to withhold. This is real victory achieved through superhuman wisdom, which God is waiting to bestow in answer to prayer (5).

Confidence in Adversity (James 1:5-12)

In verse 5 James demonstrated the grace that was working in his own soul. We all lack wisdom. Yet he does not accuse us of our ignorance. Rather he suggested that we may need help from God along this line: "If any of you lack wisdom"! Who does not realize this lack in his own life if at all characterized by the spirit of humility? But knowing our need is the first step toward receiving that which will meet the need. So we are urged to ask of God—He who is infinite in wisdom, and who delights to satisfy our need when we come to Him as children to a Father.

It is God's pleasure to give wisdom to those who ask in faith, but if we make request in a formal manner without implicit confidence in His readiness to answer we only dishonor Him and so there is no response. To ask in faith necessitates knowing that our petition is in accordance with His will. But we may be assured it is always His desire to impart to His people the necessary wisdom that will enable them to pursue a right course through this world.

To pray with hesitation or wavering is to fail of blessing. A person who doubts God is as unstable as the waves of the sea tossed around by contrary winds. The man of God is not to be inclined to change his mind often (Proverbs 24:21, KJV). He who continuously veers from one course to another only reveals his own instability and lack of a sense of being under the divine control. Paul wrote to the Galatians, "This persuasibleness cometh not of Him that calleth you" (Galatians 5:8, literal rendering). The man who habitually looks to God for guidance will be certain of his path.

A double-minded man is never sure of anything. He goes from one calling to another and from one line of service to another, like a bee or a butterfly flitting from flower to flower, never settling but supposing some other course might be better than the one he has taken. "The meek will he guide in judgment: and the meek will he teach his way" (Psalm 25:9). Changeableness is an evidence of an unsubdued will and usually of an inflated ego, which leads one to be occupied unduly with the importance of his own affairs.

Lowliness of mind is ever befitting those who profess to follow Christ who said, "I am meek and lowly in heart" (Matthew 11:29). If He gives promotion one can rejoice in His goodness, recognizing the blessing as pure grace (James 1:9). But if He permits conditions to change so that he who was well-to-do finds himself in comparative poverty, let him accept all as from the hand of Him who makes no mistakes. Man, after all, is but as grass and as the flower of the field; he soon passes from this world, no matter how high or low his lot may be for the moment. The flower may flourish for a few days and be admired by all who behold it, but the heat of the sun soon withers it and it fades and falls. Even so men may have their hours of exaltation, reveling in their riches and the privileges that wealth can give, but soon all this must come to an end. And unless they possess eternal riches laid up in Heaven they will be utterly bereft.

Verse 12 has in view the tried and tested believer who is assured of blessing as he endures grief for Christ's sake. When the temptation is over and the believer has remained steadfast to the end, he is promised the crown of life, which the Lord will give to all who have shown by their devotion to Him that they truly loved Him. This is not to be confused with eternal life, which is God's free gift to all who believe in the Lord Jesus Christ. The crown of life is reward for faithful endurance out of love for the Savior. It is the martyr's crown, as we see in Revelation 2:10, "Be thou faithful unto death, and I will give thee a crown of life."

Eternal life can never be forfeited. It is the common life of all the redeemed. Those who possess it will never perish (John 10:25-29). But the crown of life will be lost if one should prove unfaithful to the trust committed to him. So we are warned, "Hold that fast which thou hast, that no man take thy crown" (Revelation 3:11).

Holiness in Adversity (James 1:13-21)

James had written of temptation in the sense of testing, or trial (12). Next he wrote of it as incitement to sin (13-16). It is never right to attribute such temptation to the infinitely holy One, our

God who has called us to holiness of life. He cannot be tempted with evil; it is ever abhorrent to Him. Neither does He ever tempt anyone. Rather by many means He seeks to induce us to flee from temptation and to take the path of holy subjection to His will.

Jesus taught His disciples to pray, "Lead us not into temptation." That is, do not leave us to go our own dangerous way, which would expose us to grievous pressure from the enemy of our souls. Then in a moment of weakness we might fall into great sin, even as David did when he dilly-dallied at home instead of leading Israel to battle against their enemies (2 Samuel 11:1).

We are tempted, not by God, but by the strength of our own lustful desires. Being deceived by the craving for self-gratification we are in danger of yielding to temptation if we do not reckon ourselves dead to sin but alive unto God (Romans 6).

Lust lingered upon elicits positive sin, "for as [a man] thinketh in his heart, so is he" (Proverbs 23:7). Sin indulged in leads to death, for "the soul that sinneth, it shall die" (Ezekiel 18:4). In verse 15 James is establishing the same principle as is found in Romans 8:6: "to be carnally minded [or, the minding of the flesh] is death." We need to be careful that we make no mistake as to this. It is never safe to trifle with sin.

The grateful heart receives all as from God, knowing that every good and perfect gift (everything that He gives satisfies this description) comes down from Heaven, from the Father of lights (2:17). He knows what is in the darkness, but the light dwells with Him (Daniel 2:22), with whom is neither changeableness nor shadow cast by turning. Every blessing for time and eternity we owe to the unfailing goodness and unalterable purpose of grace.

Our new birth itself was the expression of His good will. He brought the Word of truth to bear upon our consciences, leading us to confess our sins and trust the Savior He provided. So we became a new offering of firstfruits, the pledge of the great harvest to be reaped in due time (18). Christ Himself, in His resurrection, is called the firstfruits of them that slept, and all His redeemed in the present age of grace make up the complete presentation of the new creation offering prior to the vast millennial ingathering (1 Corinthians 15:20-24).

As the objects of such matchless grace it is fitting that we be careful to represent aright the One to whom we owe so much. Therefore we are exhorted as beloved brethren to be quick to hear and heed the Word, and slow to express ourselves unless instructed by the Spirit of God. And above all, we are to be slow to wrath, or indignation, no matter what the provocation, for anger leading to revenge is never in accord with the righteousness of God (20). This expression ("the righteousness of God") is not used by James as it was by Paul in Romans and elsewhere. It does not have to do with that righteousness in which the justified soul stands before God, but rather the righteous character of God that leads Him to deal with sin according to its deserts.

It behooves us therefore, as children of God, to judge in ourselves every tendency to uncleanness or abundance of evil (of which our natural hearts are full), and to receive in simplicity the inner working of the Word of God (21). Through God's Word we find practical deliverance from the unholy tendencies with which we find ourselves in conflict. The salvation of the soul mentioned in verse 21 is not our redemption from the judgment our sins deserve, but it refers to the purification of our affections, which are the expression of our soul's activities.

Having been born again by the Word, as Peter also wrote (1 Peter 1:23), we are admonished to walk in obedience to the faith as revealed in the Holy Scriptures, not simply hearing the word, but making that Word our counselor. To do otherwise is but to deceive ourselves, imagining that an intellectual acquaintance with the truths of the Bible is all that is required (22).

To hear and know the will of God while not obeying it is to be like one looking at his own countenance in a mirror and then going away and forgetting his actual appearance (23-24). The Word of God is such a mirror. It was designed to show us what we are, and it thus reveals our need of practical cleansing.

In verse 25 the Word is called the "law of liberty," for it presents the principles of behavior for the new-born man. He delights to do the will of God. The Word is not therefore a ministry of condemnation as was the law to the unregenerate Israelite, but it is a rule of freedom, for he who truly knows the Lord rejoices in His service.

He is therefore not merely a hearer but a doer of the Word, and finds blessing in the path of obedience.

The word *religion* is found only five times in the New Testament, and *religious* but twice. In addition to the instances recorded in James 1:26-27, Paul used *religion* three times (Acts 26:5; Galatians 1:13-14, KJV), and Luke used the word *religious* once (Acts 13:43). Our English word *religion* comes from the Latin and literally means, "to bind back"—that is, to rebind man to God. As commonly used, it means a system of faith and practice. There are three different Greek words thus translated, one being practically synonymous with our rendering, but when Paul wrote of the Jews' religion he really meant "Judaism," and it should have been translated that way. When Luke wrote of *religious proselytes* he used a word meaning "worshipful adherents."

In these verses James used the word *threskia*, referring to religious faith, forms, and ceremonies. To be punctilious about these while failing to bridle the tongue, thus guarding against intemperate or unwise speech, is but to deceive oneself. Such religion is mere empty pretense.

The true religion—or practice of piety—before God and the Father is this: to exhibit real concern for the needy such as orphans and widows, and to walk in holy separation from all uncleanness, thereby keeping one's garments unspotted from the world (27). It is this victorious faith that James insisted upon—a faith that enables one to overcome the world and to rise above its sinful follies.

CHAPTER TWO
A MANIFESTED FAITH

This chapter readily divides into two sections: first, verses 1 to 13, and second, verses 14 to 26. In both parts James stressed the importance of reality in one's attitude toward God and His Word. He recognized the fact that many of those whom he addressed belonged to the twelve tribes of Israel, and in days gone by they had trusted in obedience to the law given at Sinai as a ground for acceptance with God. James therefore probed the consciences of these Jewish believers, in what we might think of as a roundabout way, in order to show them the foolishness of attempting to obtain a righteousness of their own through legal observances. In the second part of this chapter he exposed the error of supposing that a mere acceptance of the great outstanding facts of Christianity is a faith that saves. He who has received Christ in reality will demonstrate his faith by his works.

Let us note then how adroitly this inspired writer reveals the hidden evil of the natural heart.

The Law of Liberty (James 2:1-13)

Nothing more clearly indicates the selfishness of the human heart than the way in which we are partial to the wealthy and cultured, while neglecting or ignoring the poor and less educated. James speaks out vigorously against this tendency. Prejudice is hateful when found in the world and by those who make no Christian or other religious profession at all. It is far more despicable when seen in the sphere where men and women come together presumably to worship God.

In such gatherings there should be no place for either vulgar favor-itism of the rich or contempt for the indigent. To profess faith in the One who, although the Lord of Glory, became so poor that He had no place to lay His head, and yet to show partiality is most inconsis-tent. All are alike precious to Him, but the poor are in a very special sense the objects of His love and care.

The word *assembly* in verse 2 is better rendered "synagogue." As we have noticed already, those to whom James wrote were not separated from the synagogues of the Jews, but still met with their brethren in these centers where Moses was read and instruction was given in the Scriptures (see James' words in Acts 15:21). As we read James 2 we can see with the mind's eye the worshipers and adherents gathered in the synagogue. Suddenly there is a commo-tion as the opening door reveals the portly form of a distinguished and wealthy merchant, arrayed in costly garb and wearing a gold ring on his finger. Immediately there is a move in his direction by an attendant, or possibly one of the officials, who ostentatiously conducts the newcomer to a choice pew. He is ushered in with ev-ery evidence of respect and appreciation, as though he were actu-ally doing the assembly a favor by attending the service. Again the door is opened and there appears a timid-looking man of the poor-est laboring class, who looks diffidently about for a place where he will be hidden from observation and yet be able to hear the prayers and the reading of the Scriptures. At first no one makes a move to accommodate him; then finally someone offers him a footstool or a rear seat, which is accepted with humility on the part of the pov-erty-stricken brother. Surely God would be displeased at this show of favoritism. It would be a perfect revelation of the condition of the hearts of those in attendance. Such partiality would show that the thoughts of those so behaving were evil in that they despised the poor and honored the well-to-do.

Yet all are alike precious to God, and He has chosen the poor of this world, made wealthy by faith, as heirs of His kingdom in which all who love Him shall have part. To despise the poor is to dishonor Him who recognizes them as His own children.

How often had the rich and opulent led in opposition to the

gospel and in oppressing those in less fortunate circumstances, even dragging them before the courts in order to defraud them of what was lawfully theirs. These who trusted in their wealth and gloried in their power and influence were often blasphemers of "that worthy name" by which believers in Christ are called (7).

Jesus declared the second great commandment is "Thou shalt love thy neighbor as thyself." James designates this the royal law (8). It sums up man's responsibility to his neighbor. He who fulfills this law will love all men and look with contempt on none. Therefore, to show favoritism, preferring one person above another, is to violate the letter and spirit of this sacred precept, and so to commit sin and be convicted of the law as a transgressor. For one to pretend to be righteous before God while showing partiality is sheer folly. He has violated the law already and so he has no right to expect blessing on the ground of legal obedience.

It is not necessary to break every commandment of the law in order to stand condemned as a criminal in the sight of God. To offend in one point is to be guilty of all (10). The slightest infringement of the law indicates the self-will and insubjection of the heart. Suspend a man over a precipice by a chain of ten links; how many of these need to snap to plunge him into the abyss below? The breaking of the weakest link shatters the chain, and the man falls to his doom. The same law that forbids adultery, prohibits murder. One need not be guilty of both to be under judgment. To violate either command marks one out as a transgressor of the law. How hopeless then are the efforts of anyone that seeks to be justified on the ground of his own obedience.

But that law, so terrible to the sinner, is a law of liberty to the regenerated one, because it commands the very behavior in which the one born of God finds his joy and delight. Let the Christian then be careful that he does not act inconsistently with his profession, for "he shall have judgment without mercy, that hath shewed no mercy" (13). Under the divine government men reap as they sow. With what judgment they judge others, they are judged themselves, but "mercy rejoiceth against judgment." It is not the desire of God to deal harshly with anyone. He is ever ready to forgive and bless the one who recognizes and confesses his sin. As objects of such mercy ourselves we are called to show mercy and compassion to others, no matter how lowly their condition may be.

This leads naturally to insistence on the importance of a faith that is expressed through good works, and the rest of the chapter deals with this.

A Working Faith (James 2:14-26)

It seems to be a tendency inherent in most of us to go to extremes in matters of doctrine. This is true in regard to the question of our salvation as well as in other areas. Some insist that we are saved by character; that only as we do good works and consistently obey the law of God can we be justified. At the other extreme are those who rest solely on an historical faith for their acceptance with the Lord. They ignore the need of the inner change that the Savior described as a new birth, and which is evidenced by a life of practical righteousness.

The Holy Spirit used the apostle Paul in a special way to show the fallacy of the first of these views. He insisted that justification before God is never by the deeds of the law but by faith in Christ. James was concerned with the second error, and made it plain that the faith that saves is a faith that works, and that no one is justified before God who is not justified practically before men. What profit, he asked, if a man says he has faith and his behavior belies his profession? Is this the kind of faith that saves (14)?

He imagined a case where one of Christ's own is bereft of clothing and proper nourishment. Looking upon him in his distress a fellow Christian speaks comforting but useless words saying, "Depart in peace, be ye warmed and filled," but gives him nothing either in the way of food or clothing to alleviate his needy condition. What profit is there in mere words unaccompanied by deeds of mercy (15-16)?

In the same way James endeavored to show that faith that is divorced from works is dead, being alone. There is no work of grace in the heart where there are no acts of grace in the life. It was Robertson of Brighton who said, "No man is justified by faith, unless faith has made him just." For faith supposes a living link between the soul and God.

James pictured two men; one says to the other, "Thou hast faith, and I have works: show me thy faith without thy works"—something which cannot be done—"and I will show thee my faith by my works"—the only way one can prove to another that his faith is genuine (18).

To believe the great facts of the gospel is not enough: there must be personal commitment of the soul to Christ. Mere monotheism (belief in one God) is not saving faith. The demons believe that God is one, and shudder as they contemplate the day when they must face Him in the final judgment of the wicked dead and of fallen angels. Such belief has no saving value. Again James repeated the statement, "Faith without works is dead" (20). He then cited two Old Testament illustrations to confirm his thesis. First, the case of Abraham, the father of the faithful—what does Scripture teach concerning him? It shows us that he was justified by works when, in obedience to the command of God, he offered up Isaac his son upon the altar.

But Paul wrote plainly in Romans 4:2, "If Abraham were justified by works, he hath whereof to glory; *but not before God*" (italics added). Is there not contradiction here? Was not Luther right in declaring that this letter of James was not true—inspired Scripture but just "an epistle of straw"? Luther and many others failed to note those words, *not before God.* How was Abraham justified before God? James and Paul agree that it was when "Abraham believed God, and it was imputed unto him for righteousness" (James 2:23). But when he went to mount Moriah and there by faith offered his son upon the altar (Hebrews 11:17-19), he was justified by works before *men* as he demonstrated the reality of his profession of confidence in God and His word.

Therefore James said the scripture (found in Genesis 15:6) came to fulfillment in the demonstration of that faith Abraham had so long ago. Remember some forty years elapsed between the patriarch's justification by faith before God and his justification by works before men. We may see in Abraham's example how true it is that a man is justified by works and not by faith only. In other words, as Paul also wrote, faith worketh by love; otherwise it is not real faith at all (Galatians 5:6).

In Hebrews 11:31 we are told, "By faith the harlot Rahab perished not with them that believed not, when she had received the spies with peace." James wrote, "Likewise also was not Rahab the harlot justified by works, when she had received the messengers, and had sent them out another way?" (2:25) Her faith in the God of Israel caused her to do all she could for the protection of His servants, and secured for her the place of a wife and mother in Israel, bringing her right into the ancestral line of our Lord Jesus Christ (Matthew 1:5). It was faith alone that gave value to the works of both Abraham and Rahab. In one case we see a father about to sacrifice his son, in the other a woman betraying her country! Had they not had confidence in the living God, the perpetrators of both acts would have exposed themselves to severe condemnation.

The conclusion is clear in James 2:26, "As the body without the spirit is dead, so faith without works is dead also." Death is the separation of the spirit (the real man) from the body (the temporary tabernacle). As the preacher wrote in Ecclesiastes 12:7, "Then shalt the dust return to the earth as it was: and the spirit shall return unto God who gave it." A faith that is not demonstrated by works of righteousness and deeds of piety is as dead as the lifeless clay.

Were we to lose this second chapter of James we would lose much indeed. We need just such clear, practical instruction to save us from antinomianism and false confidence.

CHAPTER THREE
A CONTROLLING AND ENERGIZING FAITH

The faith of which James wrote is a vital force that enables a man to live triumphantly. It even gives him the ability to control that unruly member, the tongue, by means of which God is so often dishonored and our fellow-men injured. An unbridled tongue is at the bottom of much strife, both in the world and in the church. Those who profess faith in our Lord Jesus Christ, who was sinless in word as in all else, may well ponder the serious admonitions of this "tongue" chapter.

Controlling the Tongue (James 3:1-12)

In place of *masters* in verse 1 (KJV) we might better read *teachers*. To be recognized as an instructor of other people is to be in a place of great responsibility. If the teaching given out is faulty or misleading, none but God Himself can estimate the harm that may result to those who receive it. It is a serious thing indeed to attempt to influence men either for good or for evil. He to whom a ministry of teaching is committed needs to be much before God as to how he fulfills it. If he fails to teach the truth as God has revealed it in His Word he will receive a far greater condemnation than that to which his listeners are exposed. No man should therefore presume to take the place of a teacher if he has not been called by the Lord to this work and so gifted by the Holy Spirit. It is the risen Christ who has given gifts to His church, among which are "pastors and teachers"

(Ephesians 4:11). It is noticeable that the two are intimately connected. Every true pastor should be able to teach the Word in clearness and power; and every God-endowed teacher should have a pastor's heart. Otherwise he is in danger of becoming heady and high-minded, and devoting himself simply to imparting information instead of bringing the truth to bear upon the hearts and consciences of his hearers.

Admittedly, there is no perfection even among the choicest of God's children. In many things we all stumble. A person who was never guilty of a slip of the tongue would be a perfectly mature, well-balanced man. One who has never uttered a faulty expression, or given vent to an idle or vain word would be perfect in his behavior and able to restrain every unholy propensity, for there is no part of the body so difficult to control as the tongue.

Horses are held in with bit and bridle (Psalms 32:9) and so become subservient to man whose strength does not compare with theirs. Great ships are controlled and directed in whatever direction the helmsman wishes, by a very small and apparently insignificant rudder. So the tongue, seemingly so weak in itself, has power to make or break one's life and testimony. Nor can any man control it in his own strength. How many have determined never again to utter a hasty or unkind word, only to find that in a moment of thoughtlessness their best resolution has been broken by the activity of this unruly member, the tongue, whose power for good or evil is so great.

This little member is likened to a fire which, though small in the beginning, proves devastatingly ruinous as its results spread far and wide. A word has tremendous power for good or ill. The expressive illustration used in the last part of James 3:5 is often so misquoted as to miss the sense of it entirely. People say, "Behold, how great a fire a little matter kindleth!" But that is a complete perversion of the proverb—for a proverb it is. "Behold," said James, "how great a matter a little fire kindleth!" Quoted correctly, we grasp the meaning and visualize the picture at once. A tiny spark may start a conflagration that results in stupendous loss. An unwise or unkind word may be the beginning of trouble that will go on for years and be the means of unceasing strife and division.

All species and varieties of birds and beasts, even slimy serpents and creatures of the sea, have been tamed by patient handling and attention (7). But no man can tame his own tongue. It is an irrepressible rebel, an insubordinate and wicked malefactor capable of stirring men to every kind of iniquity and "full of deadly poison." We speak of a scandal-monger as having a serpent tongue, and the simile is in full accordance with the damage such an evil speaker inflicts. The amazing thing is that even after one has been brought to know the Lord, he still finds he has trouble with his tongue. This is because of the fact that the believer has two natures: the old, corrupt nature inherited from the first Adam, the head of the old creation; and the new and holy nature received from the last Adam, the Head of the new creation. Such is the power of the old nature that unless there is constant watchfulness and unceasing identification by faith with Christ in His death to sin, it will reveal itself through the tongue long after other evil inclinations have been brought under control through the power of the cross.

Who has not been shocked at times to hear the best of men and those esteemed as the holiest of saints give vent to expressions regarding fellow workmen that indicated an unsubdued nature after years of Christian experience? With the same tongue we bless God the Father and curse or injure men who are made in the image of God. Thus "out of the same mouth proceedeth blessing and cursing" (10). Surely, such things ought not so to be! When they take place it evidences a lack of communion with God and shows that the heart is, for the moment at least, uncontrolled by divine grace.

In nature we never find such an anomaly. No fountain sends forth pure and brackish water from the same vent. Trees bear according to their kind, for they have but one nature (Genesis 1:11-12). Fig trees do not produce olives, nor do grapevines bear figs. If some have fancied they have seen evidence that James' reasoning in verse 12 is faulty, and have thought they did find both fresh and salt water proceeding from the same fountain, it was because two different underground streams came to the surface very close together, but each opening poured forth only one kind of water. With the tongue it is otherwise! The same man speaks well of God and ill of man, and often fails to recognize the incongruity of such behavior.

The Two Wisdoms (James 3:13-18)

A wise man is a man of faith, a man obedient to and taught by God. Such a man will manifest his true spiritual state by good behavior. He speaks with meekness of wisdom. This will be when faith is in control and the old corrupt nature is kept in the place of death by the power of the indwelling Spirit of God. Where it is otherwise, one may well be ashamed before God and man. If bitter envying and strife are ruling in the heart it indicates an unsubdued will and a life out of harmony with God. For this there is no reasonable excuse, for abundant provision has been made in order that one may be freed from such bondage.

God waits to bestow all needed wisdom to enable us to rise triumphantly above the evil tendencies of our natural hearts. We will always fail if we seek to be guided by our own minds or by the wisdom of the flesh.

The two wisdoms stand out in vivid contrast; that which is of the earth and that which comes from Heaven (15). The former is of this world and is according to the sinful nature, which is in all men since the fall. Worldly wisdom is Satanic in origin because it is the fruit of disobedience to God from the beginning. It produces envy and strife, lack of restfulness, and every other unholy work.

In contrast to this wisdom we are exhorted to seek the wisdom that comes from Heaven, which is found in all its fullness in Christ who is Himself the Wisdom of God. He is made wisdom unto us who believe, even our sanctification and redemption. This wisdom controlling the heart and mind of the man of faith will keep the tongue from evil and the lips from speaking guile. It "is first pure"—there is no uncleanness in it; "then peaceable"—never stirring up to unholy strife; "gentle" or courteous—never biting nor sarcastic; "easy to be entreated"—not harsh and implacable; "full of mercy"—ever ready to show pity and compassion and to extend forgiveness to the repentant offender; full, too, "of good works," for a tongue controlled by divine grace can be a mighty instrument for good; "without partiality" or rather, not given to wrangling or quarreling over places of preferment, or envious because others have received recognition denied to us. Above all, or in addition to all, heavenly wisdom is "without hypocrisy" or dissimulation—absolutely honest, and speaking words that can be depended upon as truthful and sensible.

He who possesses this wisdom is enabled to control his tongue so that he sows not the thistle seed of dissension but good seed that produces righteousness. He sows in peace, because he is a man of peace, a true child of God, a peacemaker according to the words of our Lord in Matthew 5:9. When the tongue is surrendered to Christ and dominated by the Spirit it becomes one of our most useful members; when it falls under the control of the enemy it works untold grief and damage.

CHAPTER FOUR

A SUBMISSIVE FAITH

Faith is hindered by strife and contention, by prayerlessness and by worldliness. James wrote of these in Chapter 4 and showed that submission to the will of God enables one to overcome all these tendencies. Through submission to God we are enabled to walk in faith, looking to God for His guidance from day to day.

Dangers of a Self-centered Life (James 4:1-5)

Nothing is sadder than grievous misunderstandings among saints. How often whole churches are in uproar over the self-will of one or two who are quarreling over some question of precedence or manner of service! Wars and fightings or brawlings arise from the lusts that battle in our members—that is, unrestrained and unlawful desires struggling for fulfillment in our very being.

"Ye lust, and have not" (2). The natural heart is never contented. As brought out so vividly in the book of Ecclesiastes, nothing under the sun can satisfy the heart of the man who is made for eternity. "Ye [envy], and desire to have." The seemingly better fortune of others, instead of leading us to congratulate them because of what it has pleased God to give them, fills us with envy and jealousy if we are not walking in faith and in the Spirit. Then follows an unholy restlessness that produces strife and confusion. Like spoiled children we become fretful and quarrelsome; nothing pleases. We are continually looking for something new in order that we may obtain the satisfaction that always seems to elude us. We try everything else before we go to God, forgetting that He alone can meet our needs. Job's friends falsely accused him of restraining prayer (Job 15:4), but the accusation could justly be brought against us. Our Lord has commanded us to ask that we might receive (Matthew 7:7-8). We have not, because we ask not. How true this is of many of us. While God our Father has vast stores of grace and mercy that He is waiting to bestow on us, we fail to ask, and so we do not receive. We complain of living on at a "poor dying rate"; but the fault is entirely our own. We do not stir ourselves up to pray to God. And by this very spirit of prayerlessness we give evidence of the low condition into which we have fallen.

When at last we do attempt to avail ourselves of the privilege of prayer our petitions are so self-centered and so concerned about the gratification of our own desires that God cannot in faithfulness grant our requests. True prayer is not asking God to do what we want, but first of all it is asking Him to enable us to do that which He would have us do. Too often we endeavor by prayer to control God instead of taking the place of submission to His holy will. Thus we ask and receive not; because if God answered by giving what we desire we would but consume it on our lusts, or pleasures. To pray aright there must be a separated life, with God Himself before our souls as the supreme object of our affections.

Some manuscripts omit the first term *adulterers* (James 4:4, KJV) and read, "Ye adulteresses." It is as though the Lord were charging us with being like a wife who has proven herself unfaithful to her husband. It is God Himself, revealed in Christ, to whom we owe our fullest affection and allegiance. Worldliness is spiritual adultery. "The friendship of the world is enmity with God." The term *the world* refers not to the material universe, but to that ordered system that has rejected Christ. It consists of men and women under the domination of Satan, who is both the prince and the god of this world. Whosoever attempts to go on with the world in any measure is guilty of disloyalty to Him whom it has spurned and crucified. And he who determines to be a friend of the world, makes of himself an enemy of God.

Many are the warnings in Scripture against this unholy alliance of the children of God with the children of the devil. Through the history of God's dealings with His people He has always called them to holy separation to Himself. It has ever been the effort of the devil to break down this wall of separation and to lead the two groups to become so intermingled that all vital testimony for God is destroyed. It is impossible to go on in fellowship with the world and yet to walk in fellowship with God. "Can two walk together, except they be agreed?" (Amos 3:3)

James 4:5 is perhaps a bit obscure as we have it in the King James version: "Do ye think that the scripture saith in vain, The spirit that dwelleth in us lusteth to envy?" Some have thought the reference was to a part of Genesis 8:21, "The imagination of man's heart is evil from his youth." But this appears to be very far-fetched. Might we not rather read the verse as a question followed by an assertion? First, "Do ye think that the scripture speaketh in vain?" That is, can we imagine that the many warnings against worldliness found throughout Scripture are all merely empty phrases? Surely not. The Scripture speaks solemnly and definitely against this evil, and we refuse obedience at our peril. Then the last half of the verse refers to the gracious work of the Holy Spirit rather than to the restless cravings of our human spirits: "The Spirit who dwelleth in us yearns enviously." He is grieved and distressed when we prove unfaithful to the Christ who has redeemed us and to the Father who has blessed us so richly. The Holy Spirit yearns over us with a holy envy or jealousy, for our God is a jealous God. He would have us wholly for Himself. A divided allegiance means disaster in our own experience and dishonors Him who rightfully claims us as His own. We may shrink from complete surrender to His will, involving utter separation from the world, but as Augustine said, "God's commandings are God's enablings." What He requests He gives us ability to do.

Benefits of a God-centered Life (James 4:6-17)

Elsewhere we are invited to come boldly to the throne of grace, that we may find grace for help in our time of need (Hebrews 4:16). That grace is given freely to all who come to God in the spirit of self-judgment, seeking the needed strength that their behavior might glorify Him. He, whose we are and whom we should ever serve, is ready always to supply the needed strength that we may rise above the allurements of the world. But we must approach His throne in lowliness of spirit, for "God resisteth the proud, but giveth grace unto the [lowly]," as David affirmed in Psalm 138:6, and Solomon likewise in Proverbs 3:34.

As with repentant hearts we bow in submission to the will of God we obtain the grace needed to triumph over every foe. We need not even fear the great archenemy of God and men, the devil. We need not run in terror from his assaults or faint in fear when he seeks to overcome us. All we need to do is to stand firmly on the ground of redemption, resisting Satan in the power of faith. Notice how both James and Peter agree in this as they write under the guidance of the overruling Holy Spirit. James wrote, "Resist the devil, and he will flee from you" (4:7). Peter declared: "Your adversary the devil, as a roaring lion, walketh about, seeking whom he may devour: Whom resist steadfast in the faith" (1 Peter 5:8-9). By the use of the Word and in dependence on God in prayer we become impregnable against the assaults of the evil one. The old saying is true,

> Satan trembles when he sees,
> The weakest saint upon his knees.
> (William Cowper)

In John Bunyan's *Pilgrim's Progress* we read that it was at Forgetful Green that Christian was taken off guard. He was on the point of being defeated by Apollyon but when he regained the sword of the Spirit, the foe fled.

James continued his Epistle with several intensely practical admonitions. "Draw nigh to God, and he will draw nigh to you" (4:8). He never refuses to meet the one who sincerely seeks His face. Surely we can each say with David, "It is good for me to draw near to God" (Psalms 73:28). To fail to avail ourselves of this privilege is to wrong our own souls as well as to dishonor Him who invites us to draw near. But if we would approach Him we must come with clean hands and pure hearts, for He detests hypocrisy and double-mindedness.

We must come, too, with chastened spirits; so we read, "Be afflicted, and mourn, and weep: let your laughter be turned to mourning, and your joy to heaviness" (9).

We have been careless and unconcerned far too long. The place of repentance and sorrow for our many sins is a fitting position for us. God has been dishonored by our levity and worldliness; but as we take the place of confession and self-judgment before Him, He is ready to grant us forgiveness, cleansing, and strength for the conflict before us.

His promise is definite and He will never retract it. He says, "Humble yourselves in the sight of the Lord, and he shall lift you up." He will not condemn us for our past failures, for when we judge ourselves we shall not be judged (1 Corinthians 11:31). He is ever ready to reach out the hand of help when we come to the end of ourselves.

If saints are to walk together in mutual respect and fellowship there must be no indulgence in evil-speaking. So we read, "Speak not evil one of another, brethren" (11). To do so is to reflect on God Himself, who in His infinite love and mercy has received us all and put us into this place of holy fellowship one with another. He is the supreme lawgiver to whom each one is accountable. If I pass judgment on my brethren I am speaking evil of the law and therefore of the One who gave it. Each is to answer for himself before God. I cannot answer for my brother, nor he for me. We are all alike called to be doers of the law—that is, to render obedience to the Word. Evil-speaking is in itself disobedience. So if I indulge in and speak disparagingly of my brother, condemning him for disobedience, I am utterly inconsistent because I am disobedient also. Each must give account directly to God "who is able to save and to destroy" (12). What right then have I to judge another? Paul's words are apropos here, "Therefore, judge nothing before the time, until the Lord come, who both will bring to light the hidden things of darkness, and will make manifest the counsels of the hearts: and then shall every man have praise of God" (1 Corinthians 4:5). Our Lord Jesus Himself has commanded us, saying, "Judge not, that ye be not judged" (Matthew 7:1). How easily we forget such admonitions!

The closing verses of James 4 emphasize that the life of faith is one of daily dependence on the Lord. Although we know that no man can be sure of even another hour of life—let alone of days, months, and years—we still make our plans and arrangements as though we were sure of being here for years to come. It is not wrong to do this if we remember that all is in subjection to the divine will. Obviously we must look ahead and so seek to order our affairs that we can do what is right and necessary as the time goes by. But we are here warned against making such plans in independence of God. In Proverbs 27:1 we read, "Boast not thyself of tomorrow; for thou knowest not what a day may bring forth." And in James we are told, "Ye know not what shall be on the morrow" (4:14). It would seem hardly necessary to be reminded of this, and yet we forget it so readily. Our life is but as a breath. It is ours for a little time—at the most a few score years—then it vanishes away. We are the creatures of a day; yet we act as though we were going to be here forever!

God would have us dependent on Himself from day to day. In looking forward to the future we should seek to know His will. This involves, not merely writing "D. V." (*Deo Volente,* "God willing") when we suggest a date for a certain purpose, but also it implies seeking the mind of God before making any such arrangements at all. All should be subject to His will, and if He be pleased to preserve us in life here on earth. To act otherwise is to take an attitude of independence—an inappropriate attitude for those whose existence here may be terminated at any moment. To forget this and to act in pride, rejoicing in our boastings, is to dishonor God. "All such rejoicing is evil."

James closed this section of his Epistle with the serious reminder, "Therefore to him that knoweth to do good, and doeth it not, to him it is sin" (4:17). Sin is any lack of conformity to the will of God. When He makes known that will, our responsibility is to act accordingly. Otherwise we miss the mark and incur the divine displeasure. The more clearly God has revealed His mind and the better we understand it, the greater is our responsibility.

CHAPTER FIVE
A PATIENT AND EXPECTANT FAITH

The believer in Christ is a stranger and a pilgrim passing on through a world arrayed in opposition against God. He sees confusion and strife on every hand, all the result of sin and rebellion against the only One who would have brought peace to this troubled world had men but received Him when He came in humility. Because of their refusal to accept Him, wars and tumults have prevailed ever since. Men of various callings have embroiled one with another in fierce contentions. The struggle between capital and labor is pictured in the first part of the present chapter. These difficulties will never be settled satisfactorily until the Lord returns again to take His great power and reign. To this glad event faith looks on in patience and expectancy.

Warning to the Wealthy (James 5:1-6)

"Money," we are told, "answereth all things" (Ecclesiastes 10:19). But no man can be certain that his wealth will abide. It may be swept away in a most unexpected manner. The day draws near when those who trusted in their riches will weep and howl in their distress as they face multiplied misery and wretchedness, for "riches profit not in the day of wrath" (Proverbs 11:4). And "he that getteth riches, and not by right, shall leave them in the midst of his days, and at his end shall be a fool" (Jeremiah 17:11). Those who accumulate wealth by oppressing the poor and underpaying their employees will find their riches become corrupted and their costly garments moth-eaten. The gold and silver they have stored up will become corroded, and the rust will become a witness against them. It will testify to the greed and covetousness that led them to amass vast stores of money. If their hearts had been right that wealth might have been used to the glory of God in alleviating human misery, or in furthering the work of the kingdom of God.

Significantly we are told, "Ye have heaped treasure together for [or, in] the last days" (3). There is surely more than a suggestion here that just such conditions as are described will prevail to an unusually large extent as the end draws on.

No demagogic labor leader ever spoke out more strongly against unfairness to laborers than James did in these verses. Inspired by the Holy Spirit, he inveighed against such crass selfishness and cruel callousness concerning the needs of the working classes. "Behold," he exclaimed, "the hire [or wages] of the labourers who have reaped down your fields, which is of you kept back by fraud, crieth: and the cries of them which have reaped are entered into the ears of the Lord of Sabaoth"—that is, of Jehovah of hosts (4). Men may think of God as an uninterested spectator, even if He sees the wrongs inflicted by one class upon another. But it is not so. On the contrary, He is deeply concerned about all the injustice and oppression that cause such bitter suffering. Just as He heard the cries of the slaves in Egypt when they sighed and groaned because of their unfair and wicked treatment by the taskmasters of Pharaoh, so He still takes note of every wrong that the privileged and powerful inflict on the poor and downtrodden. "When he maketh inquisition for blood, he remembereth them: he forgetteth not the cry of the humble" (Psalms 9:12).

Sternly James rebuked the selfish pleasure-lovers who revel in their luxuries, while those whose toil earned the money thus squandered are living in circumstances of the most distressing character. "Ye have lived in pleasure on the earth, and been wanton," he exclaimed. Wantonness or reckless self-indulgence includes every form of lewdness and immorality and is the natural result of unfeeling callousness concerning those in less fortunate circumstances. These selfish pleasure-lovers were just like fed cattle nourished for the day of slaughter. Their doom is certain in the day of the Lord's vengeance.

Their attitude toward the poor is the same in character as the attitude of the world toward Christ: "Ye have condemned and killed the just [One]; and he doth not resist you" (6). Had they loved Him they would have loved those for whom He died, but having spurned Him we need not be surprised at their heartless indifference to the woes and griefs of those who, like Him, are despised.

The Part of Patience (James 5:7-12)

What then is the remedy that James set forth? What cure is there for all this industrial strife? Did he advocate that Christian workmen should join in association with godless confederations of laborers who know not God? Did he suggest that they should unite together and strike for the proper recognition of their just demands? Not at all, for in this case, as in all others, "the wrath of man worketh not the righteousness of God" (1:20). So James reminded the suffering children of God of the blessed hope of the Lord's return. Not until He takes over the reins of government will conditions ever be put right in this poor world. Thus he wrote exhorting to patient endurance until the coming of the Lord. He used a little parable to show that Christ Himself is the Man of patience now while He sits upon the Father's throne. The farmer plants the seed and waits in patience for the harvest, knowing there must first be the early and then latter rain before a good crop can be assured. In the same way our blessed Lord, having commissioned His servants to sow the good seed, waits expectantly at God's right hand until "the precious fruit of the earth" is ready to be garnered (7). We too are exhorted to be patient, with hearts established in grace, looking up in faith as we realize that the very conditions depicted only emphasize the fact that "the coming of the Lord draweth nigh."

As objects of grace ourselves we can well afford to show grace to others, even though they treat us despitefully. It is not for us to take judgment into our own hands; we are not to endeavor to repay in kind for the evil that unprincipled and wicked men do to us. If we attempt to revenge ourselves we shall fall under condemnation. The only One who can rightly handle these matters is the Lord Himself; as the Judge He stands at the door, waiting for the appointed time when He will deal with all who defy the divine law of love (9).

If any complain of the difficulty that is involved in patiently enduring such wrongs James points them to the prophets of God in all ages, who demonstrated patience and long-suffering while enduring the afflictions heaped on them by wicked men. If our trials seem inexplicable as we reflect on the character of God, and we find ourselves questioning how a good God can permit such pain—mental and physical—James reminds us of the patriarch Job. When he was distressed beyond measure because of the ills he had to bear he endured as seeing Him who is invisible, and cried out, "But he knoweth the way that I take: when he hath tried me, I shall come forth as gold" (Job 23:10). The purpose of the Lord was seen when Job bowed in humility of spirit before God, exclaiming, "I abhor myself, and repent in dust and ashes" (Job 42:6). Well may we take Job as our example, and see too in the Lord's final dealings with His poor troubled servant that He "is very pitiful and of tender mercy." Our real victory is found in that self-abasement that justifies God and condemns ourselves.

It is not fitting that poor frail mortals such as we, make strong assertions bound by oaths in which we use the sacred name of God and His heavenly abode or even the earth He has created. In James 5:12 we have an echo of our Savior's words as found in Matthew 5:34-37. Oaths of every kind are forbidden. They not only dishonor God and His creation, but also they are most unbecoming on the lips of those who are finite creatures, whose every breath depends from one moment to another on the mercy of the Lord.

The Prayer of Faith (James 5:13-20)

James continued by admonishing the afflicted to seek recourse in prayer, assured that God's ear is ever open to our cry. If any are merry—that is, cheerful of heart—let them sing, not the frivolous, empty songs of the world, however beautiful the melodies to which they are set, but psalms, sacred songs of praise, the expressions of a soul that finds its joy in God.

James 5:14-16 brings before us faith's resource in times of illness. This passage has been the subject of considerable controversy and is admittedly difficult to understand. We must keep in mind the special character of this Epistle as a last message to the twelve tribes, as such, before the complete separation of Christianity from Judaism, which the Epistle to the Hebrews insists upon. God, in condescending grace, meets people where they are and this is a case in point.

When the twelve apostles went out to the lost sheep of the house of Israel, they anointed the sick with oil, and God granted healing in response to their faith (Mark 6:13). This is the only other instance in the New Testament where this method is said to have been employed. It is significant because of its definite connection to the testimony to Israel. There may be some truth in the view some have held that the oil was in itself a healing ointment, and that God blessed the means used in connection with the recovery of those who were ill. But James specifically declared, "The prayer of faith shall save the sick;" though this would not necessarily mean that any virtue residing in the oil itself was ignored, as God often answers prayer by blessing the means used.

The sick were to call for the elders of the church or the assembly. In the present broken condition of things in the church it might be difficult to say just who these elders are. In the beginning it was a simple matter. Elders were appointed in every church either by direct apostolic authority or by apostolic delegates, as in the instances of Timothy and Titus. It seems that where this special oversight was not available, assemblies appointed their own elders in accordance with the instructions given in the pastoral Epistles. With no direct apostolic authority today, following these instructions is all that can be done. But are these recognized brethren actually elders of *the* church? One does not want to raise needless questions, but in the endeavor to carry out the instructions in James literally in this day of ruin, they need to be faced honestly.

Throughout Scripture oil is the type or symbol of the Holy Spirit; in connection with prayer for the sick this symbolism has a beautiful significance. But whether any feel free to use oil in this way

now or not, it is always right for godly elder brethren to meet with
the sick for prayer, and it is just as true now as in the beginning of
the dispensation that God answers the prayer of faith.

In the case brought before us in James 5 it seems to be taken for
granted that the illness is part of divine chastening because of sins
committed. Therefore when the sick one called for the elders it would
in itself be his acknowledgment of his failure. It is not said, however, as Rome would have us believe, that he confessed his sins to
the elders. He confessed to God, and if to man also (as in verse 16),
it was not as recognizing any special sacerdotal authority on the
part of the elders.

It is important also to observe that in the Greek manuscript two
very different words are used for the English word *sick*. "Is any sick
among you?" (14) Here the word means "ill," as with some disease.
But where we read, "The prayer of faith shall save the sick" (15),
the word means "weak," or "exhausted." It might refer to mental
depression such as often accompanies illness, particularly when one
is conscious that he is afflicted because of his own sins and indis-
cretions.

"If he have committed sins, they shall be forgiven him" (15).
This has to do with the authority of God in His own family (see 1
Peter 1:17). The Father judges according to the behavior of His
children. When in answer to the prayer of faith the depression of
spirit is relieved and the sick one raised up, he may have the assur-
ance of God's governmental and restorative forgiveness.

In the early days of what is now generally known as "the Brethren Movement," Mr. J. N. Darby and Mr. J. G. Bellett were called
in to many sick rooms in Dublin, where they acted literally upon
the directions given in James 5:14-15. Many remarkable healings
were granted in answer to the prayer of faith; so much so that attention began to be centered upon these two brethren as special instru-
ments used of God. This attention troubled them and they felt it
wise to desist from going to the sick, but prayed together or sepa-
rately for the afflicted in a more private way, acting rather on verse
16 than on verses 14 and 15. God answered in the same grace as
when the formal service was carried out.

This is ever faith's resource. Burdened hearts can and should confess their sins one to another when conscious that their illness is chastening for wrong done against the Lord. Then we can pray one for another that healing may follow: for the earnest prayer of a righteous man is ever effective.

A Roman priest pointed to this scripture when insisting that it taught confession to one of his order. His hearer responded, "I will confess my sins to you if you will confess yours to me." He refused to recognize the mutual confession here enjoined. There is nothing official or priestly about the command in James 5:16.

Then again, there is no authority here for the Romanist "sacrament of extreme unction," which consists of anointing with consecrated oil one who is about to die. But in these verses the anointing is in view of the sick man's coming back to health, not preparation for death. So readily do Roman apologists seize on the most unlikely passages to bolster up their unscriptural practices and superstitious theories!

Next James introduced Elijah as an illuminating example of the effectiveness of fervent prayer (17-18). We are apt to think of prophets and other servants of God mentioned in the Bible as men who were of a different fiber than we are. But they were all of the same family of frail humanity, men of like passions with us, but men who dared to believe God and to give Him full control of their lives. In answer to Elijah's earnest prayer there was no rain in the land of Israel for three-and-a-half years, until godless Ahab was brought to utter despair. Then when the prophet prayed at mount Carmel there was "a sound of abundance of rain" bringing gladness to the hearts of men and refreshment to the parched earth (1 Kings 18:41-45). Comment is needless. The story points its own moral.

The Epistle of James closes rather abruptly, as we might think, with a word of encouragement for any who might be used of God to help restore an erring brother (19-20). The sinning one here, as in verse 15, is a believer who has gone astray from the path of subjection to the truth. To patiently go after such an one and to convert, or turn him again, to obedience to the Lord is to save a soul from death—physical death, which is the last act of God in His government of

His family—and to cover or hide a multitude of sins. This is to practice the love that Peter also tells us "shall cover the multitude of sins" (1 Peter 4:8), not our own sins of course, but those of the erring brother. By leading him to repentance, so that he judges himself and acknowledges his waywardness, he is restored to fellowship with God and preserved from going deeper into sin. If he were to continue in his sin the heavy hand of the Lord would have to be upon him in further chastening, even to shortening his life on earth as an evidence of the divine displeasure. This is the same as sinning unto death in 1 John 5:16-17. Many a child of God has been taken home far earlier than he would otherwise have been, because of willfulness and insubjection of spirit.

In closing our study of this most practical Epistle let us emphasize anew the great importance of a faith that works—a faith that is evidenced by a life of devotion to the Lord and of concern for the welfare of our brethren in Christ particularly and for all men generally.

FIRST PETER

FIRST PETER
SALVATION AND SUFFERING

BY JOHN PHILLIPS

Practical advice concerning the salvation and the behavior of the Christian is the emphasis of the two Epistles known to the church today as the first and second Epistles of the apostle Peter.

The writer of the first of the two Epistles that today bear Peter's name is unquestionably Peter, the great apostle of the Gospels and of the book of Acts. This first Epistle of Peter was written from Babylon (5:13) and was addressed to "the strangers scattered abroad throughout Pontus, Galatia, Cappadocia, Asia, and Bithynia" (1:1), regions forever associated with the ministry of the apostle Paul. From the emphasis on suffering in the Epistle it appears that the Jewish believers who were especially on Peter's heart were in the midst of persecution for their faith in Christ. Peter showed that Christ is our example in suffering and the certainty of our hope of glory. The latter part of the seventh decade of the first century A.D. was certainly one of terrible persecution.

Peter said that he was in Babylon (5:13). That is not surprising. Babylon was still a great city. There were a million Jews in Babylon in early New Testament times—they had been there since the Babylonian captivity. When in the days of Zerubbabel, Ezra, and Nehemiah the remnant came back to lay claim to the promised land in view of the coming of Christ, the majority of Jews stayed behind. Like many American Jews today, quite willing to support the state of Israel with their money and their influence but not willing to go there to live, many Babylonian Jews elected to stay where they were. Business was good, and the political atmosphere was congenial—why go roughing it in the promised land? Why deliberately court hardship and danger?

Peter was the apostle to the Jews. So, when he said that he was in Babylon, we can take it he was in Babylon. There are those who say that when Peter wrote "Babylon" he meant "Rome." It is true that when John wrote about "Babylon" in Revelation 17 he meant Rome, but that is because he was writing about "mystery Babylon," the Roman church in its full and final development—heir and successor of Babylonian religion, power, worldliness, and pride. In any case, John left enough clues in the chapter to enable us to identify the city of which he was writing as Rome. It is a different matter in Revelation 18, where the symbolic gives way to the literal and where Babylon is Babylon—a literal city, the rebuilt Babylon of the beast's tomorrow.

Many who claim that when Peter wrote "Babylon" he actually meant "Rome" have a vested interest in putting Peter at Rome. They want to make him the first pope. The "Historical Index" at the back of the Roman Catholic Bible, under the date A.D. 39, says: "He [St. Peter] is thought to have gone about this time to Antioch in Syria, and to have founded the episcopal see [of Antioch]." The generally received account among Roman Catholics, and one that can claim a long traditional acceptance, is that Peter came to Rome in the second year of Claudius (that is, A.D. 42), and that he held the see twenty-five years. The "Historical Index," under the date A.D. 68, says: "About this time St. Peter and St. Paul came to Rome....[Not] long after, they were both put in prison, and suffered martyrdom."

Since so many millions of people take these bald and unsupported statements at their face value, we need to put them to the test. We will first take up the claim that Peter founded the episcopal see of Antioch and was its bishop from A.D. 39 until A.D. 44. Here are the Biblical facts:

1. Three years after Paul's conversion Peter was living in Jerusalem (A.D. 38-40) (Galatians 1:15-18).
2. Then he was at Lydda (Acts 9:26-32).
3. Next at Joppa (Acts 10).
4. Then at Caesarea (Acts 10).
5. Next we find him back at Jerusalem (Acts 11:2).
6. He was imprisoned in Jerusalem by Herod Agrippa I (A.D. 44) (Acts 12).

So Peter seems to have had little time for his supposed bishopric.
As to the claims that he was bishop of Rome beginning with A.D. 42, the following Biblical facts make it virtually impossible:

1. In A.D. 44 Peter was in prison in Jerusalem (Acts 12).
2. He was a prominent member of the Council of Jerusalem in A.D. 49 (Acts 15).
3. Soon afterwards he was at Antioch, where Paul rebuked him for dissembling and dividing the church (Galatians 2).
4. Paul wrote his Epistle to the Romans in A.D. 56. The Epistle makes no mention of Peter and contains no apology for interfering in the sphere of another apostle's labors. On the contrary, Paul said that he would not "build upon another man's foundation" (Romans 15:20). There is no hint in Romans of anything like an apostolic visit to Rome by Peter or any other apostle hitherto. Paul was evidently looking forward to his own proposed visit as being an occasion when the Roman church would receive spiritual gifts lacking at the time he wrote.
5. In the same Epistle, Paul greeted two dozen people by name. The name of Peter is conspicuously absent.
6. Paul arrived in Rome in chains in A.D. 58-59 and was met by many leading believers. Again no mention was made of Peter (Acts 28).
7. The Jews at Rome seem to have been singularly ignorant of the truths of Christianity (Acts 28). That hardly seems evidence of Peter's by now supposed seventeen-year

residence in the city as its chief bishop, especially when he was specifically commissioned to be the apostle to the Jews.

8. While a prisoner at Rome (A.D. 59-61) Paul wrote four Epistles (Philippians, Colossians, Philemon, and Ephesians) and named numerous people who were his helpers in the work in the city. No mention was made of Peter, which to say the least, would have been very strange if Peter was indeed bishop of Rome.

9. Paul was back in Rome expecting martyrdom in A.D. 68 or thereabouts and wrote his last letter (2 Timothy). Not only did he not mention Peter, he stated: "Only Luke is with me" (4:11). He said that at his first trial "no man stood by me, but all men forsook me. I pray God that it might not be laid to their charge" (4:16). Are we to suppose that Peter, if he were bishop of Rome, would have deserted Paul?[1]

In the light of Biblical evidence, it is very difficult to support the idea that Peter was bishop of Rome from A.D. 42 to A.D. 68. It is not at all certain he was ever there at all. In 1 Peter he said he was at Babylon. Evidently he was ministering to the church in that city, though he was writing to churches in far-off Pontus, Galatia, Cappadocia, Asia, and Bithynia—in other words, to churches pioneered by Paul.

Something must have prompted the writing of 1 Peter. Why should Peter feel the compulsion of the Holy Spirit to write to the "elect sojourners of the dispersion" (as he calls them in the literal translation of 1:1)? The persons he addressed were doubtless Christian Jews scattered abroad throughout the Roman Empire. And why should he write to Jews and Gentiles in areas of the Roman Empire he himself had seemingly never visited?

In the first place, his name would be well-known to all Christians. It was a name that carried tremendous weight in the early church. After all, Peter was one of the very chiefest of the apostles. He had been an intimate, personal follower of the Lord Jesus when Jesus had lived on earth. A letter from Peter would be read and prized by Christians everywhere. But why did he write—and when?

The letter seems to have been written between A.D. 63 and 67. So it was written during that first great persecution of the church instigated by Nero. That persecution started in November 64 and lasted until Nero's death in A.D. 68. This was a widespread persecution, not confined to Rome but extending more or less over the whole empire. It was one of the most savage and terrible persecutions in all the church's long and checkered history.

There are many clues that this persecution was raging when this letter was penned. Peter spoke of the "trial of your faith, being much more precious than of gold that perisheth, though it be tried with fire" (1:7). He said: "Beloved, think it not strange concerning the fiery trial [the word has to do with burning and with a furnace] which is to try you [literally, 'the burning which is taking place among you']" (4:12). All the way through the Epistle we have references to terrible, false accusations being made against the Christians. There are exhortations such as: "Be not afraid of their terror." This then is the background of the Epistle. Nero's persecutions! What a flood of light that casts on this letter. It should be read in that light.

First Peter deals with salvation, Scripture, sanctification, separation, submission, suffering, shepherding, and Satan.

    I. INTRODUCTION (1:1-2)
   II. THE QUESTION OF SALVATION (1:3-9)
  III. THE QUESTION OF SCRIPTURE (1:10-12)
  IV. THE QUESTION OF SANCTIFICATION (1:13-25)
   V. THE QUESTION OF SEPARATION (2:1-12)
  VI. THE QUESTION OF SUBMISSION (2:13–3:13)
 VII. THE QUESTION OF SUFFERING (3:14–4:19)
VIII. THE QUESTION OF SHEPHERDING (5:1-7)
  IX. THE QUESTION OF SATAN (5:8-11)
   X. CONCLUSION (5:12-14)

Our salvation includes three elements: an expectant hope (1:3-4), an experiential faith (1:5-7), and an expressive love (1:8-9). So, come what may, the end is bound to be "joy unspeakable and full of glory" (1:8). Persecution should not deter us, for did not the prophets of old diligently inquire into the Scriptures that came from their pens, seeking to understand "the sufferings of Christ, and the glory that should follow" (1:11)? Moreover, the angels desire to gaze into those things of which believers have become partakers. Therefore, the child of God must be holy. Peter contrasted "the former lusts" (1:14) with the family likeness (1:15) and went on to show that believers are "born again, not of corruptible seed, but of incorruptible, by the word of God, which liveth and abideth for ever" (1:23). Separation is essential to live a holy life. As newborn babes we are separated from the past habits of sin by birth (2:1-3); as living stones we are separated from the past habits of sin by belief (2:4-10); and as strangers and pilgrims we are separated from past habits of sin by behavior(2:11).

Submission is an essential ingredient in the Christian life, whether it be as subjects of the state, servants of a master, or saints of the Lord. We should submit even if suffering is entailed, for "Christ also suffered for us, leaving us an example, that ye should follow his steps" (2:21). An important section of the Epistle deals specifically with the whole question of suffering. Peter showed that it will be experienced (3:14-17), for being a Christian does not exempt one from suffering. That was exemplified at Calvary (3:18-22). The Christ who allows us to suffer has Himself suffered and carried the whole experience right through to victory at God's right hand. Suffering indeed is to be expected (4:1-2), but it has an explanation (4:3-6) and can be exploited (4:7-11). Indeed, suffering was actually exalted by Peter, for he showed it to be a means of winning glory (4:12-14). Finally, Peter examined suffering and gave various reasons for it (4:15-19).

Peter closed his Epistle with exhortations to the shepherds of the flock and with warnings about Satan. The twin themes of suffering and glory run throughout the Epistle, Peter describing himself as "a witness of the sufferings of Christ, and also a partaker of the glory" (5:1). In contrast with Peter, Paul was a witness of the glory and a partaker of the sufferings. In some measure every believer is called to share with Christ in both.

1. Peter's first Epistle strikes at the roots of many of the cherished dogmas of Rome, as do Peter's other writings and speeches. They strike at Rome's claim that Peter was the rock on which the church was built (2:6); Rome's historic suppression of the Scriptures (2:2); Rome's claim that we should pray to Mary rather than directly to God (1:17); Rome's sale of indulgences (1:18); Rome's claim that the Scriptures are to be supplemented by tradition (1:18); Rome's teaching that salvation is by works (2:24); Rome's craving for temporal power (2:13-17); Rome's hierarchy of one man lording power over the church (5:3-4); Rome's practice of giving her priests special status over others (2:5-9); Rome's claim that only ordained people can minister (4:10-11); Rome's desire for money (5:2; Acts 3:6); Rome's desire for adulation of men (5:6); Rome's concept of baptismal regeneration (3:20-21).

INTRODUCTION

The Epistles of Peter were written primarily—in accord with his special ministry to the circumcision (Galatians 2:8)—to Christian Jews of the dispersion, who lived in various provinces in western Asia, where most of the apostle's labors had been. The letters deal with the believer's relation to the kingdom of God rather than to the church as the body of Christ; though, of course, those to whom he wrote were, as are all Christians, members of the church and subjects of the kingdom. Both letters are wilderness Epistles; they contemplate the children of God, not in their heavenly aspect as in Ephesians (1:3; 2:6), but rather as strangers and pilgrims journeying on through the wilderness of this world from the cross to the Glory.

Peter explained that he wrote the first letter to testify that "this is the true grace of God wherein ye stand" (1 Peter 5:12) . This grace is not so much the grace that saves (as in Romans 5:1-2), which gives us a perfect standing before the throne of God. Rather Peter wrote of the grace ministered to us day by day, which enables us to stand against all the wiles of the enemy and despite all the trials of the way. Suffering has a large place in the Epistle. It is perceived as normal for the believer to undergo affliction while pressing on to the inheritance laid up for him in Heaven. In this we are reminded of Savonarola's words, "A Christian's life consists in doing good and suffering evil." He is to rejoice for the privilege of suffering for Him who has redeemed us with His own blood.

The mystery of suffering has perplexed many all down through the ages. It is part of man's sad inheritance because of sin having come into the world, and in this life the child of God is not exempt from pain, sorrow, and anguish. But the suffering of believers is all ordained of God to work out for blessing. Through this ministry of suffering we are enabled to understand better what our Lord went through for us when in this world. He was "a man of sorrows, and acquainted with grief" (Isaiah 53:3). God uses suffering to keep us from sin (1 Peter 4:1; 2 Corinthians 12:7), and as a means of chastening and discipline whereby we are made more like our blessed Lord (Hebrews 12:6-11). As we suffer because of faithfulness to His name and devotion to His cause, we enjoy a very real sense of fellowship with Him who is still hated by the world that rejects His testimony. The reward is sure and will make us forget all our light affliction in the enjoyment of the eternal weight of glory (2 Corinthians 4:17).

Christians are not exempt from suffering. When one trusts in Christ, it does not mean that he is at once freed from all the consequences of sin. So far as divine judgment is concerned, he is forever delivered from that (John 3:18); but he is still in the body from which the Adamic curse has not yet been lifted. Consequently he suffers with the groaning creation of which that body is still a part. Then in addition to this, he now finds that the world to which he once belonged, has now become a scene of hostility because of his association with a rejected Christ. All this involves suffering, but with every trial and affliction there will come needed grace to endure, "as seeing him who is invisible" (Hebrews 11:27).

There is a difference between suffering with Christ (Romans 8:17) and suffering for Him (Acts 5:41). All Christians suffer with Him because of the very fact that they are partakers of the divine nature, and therefore are quick to feel the adverse conditions through which they are called to pass. But to suffer for Him is to bear shame and reproach—even unto persecution and death—for Christ's name (Acts 9:16).

The apostle Paul wrote in Galatians 2 that after consultation with the leaders at Jerusalem, following his conversion, it was arranged among them that Peter should go especially to the Jews and he to the Gentiles. It was not that either confined himself to one particular class, but He that worked mightily through Peter in the conversion of the Jews worked in the same way through Paul in bringing the men of the nations to Christ. In his letters Peter still has particularly in view his brethren after the flesh—the dispersed of Israel—scattered among the nations and living in the countries mentioned in the opening verse of 1 Peter. These were Jews generally known as the *diaspora*. While away from the land of Palestine they still looked upon it as their native country, until they gave up their earthly standing to become members of a new and redeemed nation, whose inheritance was laid up in Heaven. To them Peter wrote, encouraging them to trust in the Lord and go on in patience even in the midst of suffering. Of this he had much to say in his letter. It is an Epistle for afflicted believers, for while addressed primarily to Hebrew Christians, it was no more confined to them than Paul's letters addressed to churches among the Gentiles are to be considered as only for those who, by nature, were strangers to the covenant of promise. In Christ there is neither Jew nor Gentile, so what is written to one is intended for the help and instruction of all those who are born again.

First Peter is characteristically a wilderness Epistle. It pictures believers as journeying on from the place of the blood-sprinkling to the inheritance in Heaven, or from the cross to the Glory. Many illustrations are drawn from Israel's journey from Egypt to Canaan. In Ephesians, believers are viewed as already over the Jordan and in the promised land, enjoying their inheritance in Christ in the heavenlies. In First Peter, they are seen as a pilgrim people, strangers passing through an unfriendly world, moving on to the land of promise.

We are not able to decide exactly when First Peter was written, but it was evidently well on to the close of Peter's life. Since he himself connects the two Letters so intimately (2 Peter 3:1), they were probably not written very far apart. The date given by Ussher is A.D. 60, but there is no proof that it was as early as that. The best authorities suggest that the first Epistle was written somewhere about A.D. 66 or 67, and the second somewhat later. It is evident from 2 Peter 3:15-16 that all of Paul's Epistles were in circulation already and recognized as Scripture before Peter wrote his second letter, and we may conclude that the first one was not penned very much earlier.

This first letter readily lends itself to the following outline:

In the Wilderness with God

1 Peter	1:1-2	The Salutation
	1:3-12	The Trials of the Way
	1:13-25	Redemption and New Birth
	2:1-10	A New Nation
	2:11-25	The Pilgrim Character
	3:1-7	The Christian Family
	3:8-22	Suffering for Righteousness' Sake
	4:1-11	The New Life Contrasted with the Old
	4:12-19	Suffering as a Christian
	5:1-4	The End of the Way
	5:5-14	Grace Operative on the Journey

The following is a suggestive outline on the special theme of suffering:

Suffering as a trial of faith (1:6-7)
Christ's predicted sufferings (1:11)
Suffering for conscience' sake (2:19)
Christ's suffering, our example (2:21-23)
Suffering for righteousness' sake (3:14)
Christ suffered for our sins (3:18)
Suffering to cease from sin (4:1)
Partakers of Christ's sufferings (4:13)
Suffering as a Christian (4:16)
Suffering for a limited time (5:10)

THE PILGRIM JOURNEY

In the opening verses we have the apostolic salutation. Peter had been commissioned by the risen Christ to feed and shepherd the sheep and lambs of His flock (John 21:15-17). He addressed his letters to those who in years gone by were as sheep without a shepherd. They had been scattered on every high hill, but now had come under the loving care of the great Shepherd who appointed under-shepherds to minister to their peculiar needs.

The Salutation (1 Peter 1:1-2)

Peter addressed his Letter, "To the strangers scattered." In accordance with the Lord's instruction, Peter desired to feed and care for these scattered sheep of the house of Israel, dispersed among the nations. The lands mentioned in verse 1 are all in what we call Asia Minor, north of Palestine and Syria, and south of the Black sea. In these countries many Jews were living who had been brought to know Christ through the ministries of both Paul and Peter. They had lost their old standing as Israelites in the flesh, part of an elect nation, which however had failed so grievously. Now, through infinite grace they belonged to a new country, and were "elect according to the foreknowledge of God the Father."

There is nothing fatalistic or arbitrary about election as taught in the Scriptures. The gospel is to be preached to all, and all who believe it may be assured that they are numbered among the elect. Through the Spirit's sanctification—that is, His separating work, men are awakened and brought to see their need of Christ. When in the obedience of faith they appropriate the privilege of finding shelter beneath the sprinkled blood of Jesus they are forever safe from the judgment which their sins deserve. They are like the people of Israel on the Passover night in Egypt, who were safe within the houses, protected by the blood of the lamb sprinkled on the door-posts and lintels. God said, "When I see the blood, I will pass over you" (Exodus 12:13). So today, all who are sheltered by the blood of sprinkling may be assured that they stand where the wrath of God will never reach them.

It was to such as these that Peter wrote, wishing that grace and peace might be multiplied to them. It was not the grace that saves which he had in view, but the grace that keeps. Nor was it peace with God of which he wrote, but the peace of God which garrisons the hearts of all who learn to commit their way unto the Lord.

The Trials of the Way (1 Peter 1:3-12)

This section constitutes the introduction to the Epistle and gives us the key to the understanding of all that follows. It is noticeable how closely the words of verse 3 are linked to Ephesians 1:3. Both begin in exactly the same way, by blessing or extolling the God and Father of our Lord Jesus Christ. But as the passages in the two Epistles continue they unfold altogether different aspects of truth. In Ephesians the believer is seen as seated in the heavenlies in Christ. This is the New Testament antitype of Canaan, the inheritance which is ours already. On the other hand, Peter described the believer as journeying on to Canaan rest, which is at the end of the way. Both aspects are true and the one never contradicts the other. As to our standing we are in Christ in the heavenlies; as to our state we are pilgrims marching on to glory.

Ours is a living hope in contrast to Israel's dead hope because of their failure to fulfill the terms of the covenant entered into at Sinai. Our confidence rests not on any ability of our own to carry out certain promises, but is according to the abundant mercy that God has bestowed on us, and which is assured to us by the resurrection of Jesus Christ from the dead.

We are not seen here as already in the enjoyment of our inheritance, but we are journeying on toward it. It is reserved in Heaven for us. Unlike Canaan it is incorruptible and undefiled and shall never fade away. Even after Israel entered the land of promise they defiled it by their idolatry, and it became corrupted because of their gross wickedness so that eventually they lost it altogether. It is far otherwise with our heavenly inheritance. It is being kept for us, and we are kept for it—"kept by the power of God through faith unto salvation" in its complete and final sense. It will be revealed in the last time—that is, when we reach the end of the wilderness journey. It is not the salvation of the soul of which he speaks here. That is ours already, as we shall see in verse 9. Salvation in its complete sense includes the redemption of the body.

In view of this blessed hope we are enabled to rejoice even though "now for a season, if need be, [we] are in heaviness" of spirit because of the many trials to which we are exposed (1:6). There is a "need be" for every sorrow that the Christian is called to endure. Are we willing to trust the wisdom of God and to allow Him to plan our lives as He sees fit? Faith must be tested, otherwise it could not be verified. So we need not fear when our faith is exposed to trial that it indicates any displeasure on God's part toward us. Rather it indicates His deep interest in and concern for us. For just as gold is tried in the fire in order to separate it from the dross, so faith, which is much more precious than gold that perishes, must be tested in order that it may be found unto praise and honor and glory at the revelation of Jesus Christ from Heaven.

Precious is one of Peter's special words. He writes of the precious trial of faith (1 Peter 1:7), the precious living Stone (2:4,7), precious faith (2 Peter 1:1), and precious promises (1:4). Do we appreciate all these precious things enough to suffer for them if we are called to do so? Are we as ready to suffer for the sake of our blessed Lord as we are to profit by His sufferings on our behalf? Even the philosophic worldling can endure suffering without complaining, but it is only the regenerated one who can glory in tribulation. Just as gold is purified by the fire that consumes the dross, so God uses trial and suffering to separate the believer from those things that hinder fellowship with God and growth in the spiritual life.

Faith endures, we are told elsewhere, "as seeing him who is invisible" (Hebrews 11:27). So although we have never seen our blessed Lord with our mortal eyes, we love Him and believing in Him we rejoice with unspeakable gladness and exalted joy. The expression "full of glory" (1 Peter 1:8) is a peculiar idiom suggesting an exaltation beyond our power to express. What rapture fills the heart that is really enthralled with the unseen Christ in whom we have put our confidence, so that even here and now we know we have the salvation of our souls! We know this on the authority of the Word of God.

The prophets of ancient times spoke and wrote of this salvation; but it was not given to them to know the fullness of grace as it has now been revealed to us. They wrote as the Spirit directed concerning "the sufferings of Christ, and the glory that should follow," but they had no way of knowing the exact time when these things were to be fulfilled. Nor could they see the long period (this entire present age) that was to elapse between the cross and the glory of the Redeemer.

It was revealed to those ancient prophets that their message had to do with a future day. What they reported by the Spirit's inspiration is now the basis of our confidence and the first source of information for those who have preached the gospel in our day. They preach in the energy of the Holy Spirit who was sent down from Heaven at Pentecost to bear witness to these truths—things that had been hidden even from the angels, and which they now delight to look into. They are learning the wisdom of God in us, as we are told in Ephesians 3:10.

Redemption and New Birth (1 Peter 1:13-25)

Just as Israel was redeemed by the blood of the lamb on the night of the Passover in Egypt, and that date became to them the beginning of months when they were born as a nation, so Peter asked us to consider the marvelous realities of our redemption and our new birth.

God's word to Israel, as given in Exodus 12, was that they were to eat the Passover with their loins girded and their shoes on their feet, ready to begin their journey to the promised land the moment the signal was given to evacuate Egypt. So Peter, in addressing these sojourners in a world to which they no longer belonged, urged them to gird up the loins of their minds—that is, bring every thought into subjection to the revealed will of God, for we are to have the loins girt about with truth (Ephesians 6:14). Sobriety is to characterize God's people, for it is a serious thing to be called out of this world to live for God in the very scene where once we dishonored His name. Hope is to be the guiding pillar that leads us on to the end of the journey, which will come when Jesus Christ is revealed from Heaven (1:13).

No longer are we to conduct ourselves or fashion our behavior as we once did when in the days of our blindness and ignorance we were under the domination of carnal desires. The blue border that fringed the Israelite's garment was a reminder to him that he was linked up with the God of Heaven. As he looked upon that border he remembered that he was called to exhibit the heavenly character, for God had said, "Be ye holy; for I am holy." In the same way we are to manifest holiness in all our words and ways as becomes a heavenly people passing through a world of sin. Neither carelessness nor indifference is appropriate for those who through infinite grace are privileged to call God "Father." Rather we are to display reverent fear, lest we grieve His heart and reflect discredit upon His name.

We have been redeemed, not like Israel when they paid down the half-shekel of silver as a ransom for their souls (Exodus 30:12-15). Nor were we purchased with gold so often demanded as a ransom by some victorious leader when he dictated terms of peace to a conquered people. But we have been purchased and freed from judgment by the precious blood of Christ, and should no longer conform to the empty behavior of the past, which while in accordance with ancestral customs was opposed to the ways that glorify God. Christ was the true, unblemished and spotless paschal Lamb—free from sin or fault of any kind, either inwardly or outwardly. God had foreknown Him before the universe was created, because redemption was no after-thought with Him, hastily arranged to patch up a wrecked world ruined by man's sin and rebellion against his Creator. All had been foreseen and prepared beforehand. God had not been outwitted by Satan. It was not however until man had been tested fully under various dispensations and proven to be utterly helpless to deliver himself, that the remedy God had provided—the Savior He had foreknown—was revealed. Through Him the Father is now made known in the fullness of His grace, and by Him we believe in God who raised His blessed Son from the dead after He had finished His redemptive work. He then glorified Him by seating Him as Man at His own right hand, that our faith, or confidence, and our hope might be in God—the God of resurrection.

Redemption is a work that was accomplished by Christ Jesus on Calvary, and is therefore, so far as we are concerned, entirely objective. We could have no part in it except that we committed the sins that made it necessary, unless we had been left to die in our iniquities. But regeneration, or new birth, is subjective. Peter next speaks of this work done in us by the Word and the Spirit of God (22-23).

A great change has taken place within the hearts of all those who have obeyed the truth through the Spirit. The Word of God has been brought home to their souls in the convicting and convincing energy of the Holy Spirit, thus producing a new life and nature. The characteristic feature of this new nature is love—the love of God shed abroad in our hearts by the Holy Spirit who is given unto us (Romans 5:5). This produces love for our brethren in Christ, a love that is unselfish and pure, not contaminated by the evil desires of the flesh. For all who believe in Christ are born again—not a birth according to the natural order, not of corruptible seed; for "that which is born of the flesh is flesh," as Jesus told Nicodemus (John 3:6). But this new birth is, as we have seen, the result of believing the Word of God that liveth and abideth forever. And this Word, we are told in verse 25, is that which is proclaimed by the gospel.

Verse 24, and the first part of verse 25 are parenthetical and emphasize the contrast between that which is human and that which is divine. Peter quoted a portion of Isaiah 40:6-8 declaring that all flesh is as grass and all the glory of man as the flower of grass, which appears beautiful and verdant for a brief season and then is gone forever. For the grass soon withers and the lovely flowers fade and fall; but the Word of the Lord endures forever.

Theologians may wrangle about the necessity of a new birth by the sovereign act of God whereby the elect are first quickened and then enabled to believe unto salvation; but Scripture is clear that new birth is by means of the Word, which the Spirit of God brings to bear on the heart and conscience. Apart from this there is no divine life. James also tells us that, "Of his own will begat he us with the word of truth" (James 1:18). Believing the gospel we become children of God, and are responsible to walk as such, relying upon the Lord from day to day as we pursue our pilgrim course from the cross to the glory yet to be revealed.

CHAPTER TWO

THE PILGRIM'S CONDUCT

Just as Israel went down into Egypt as a family of seventy souls and emerged from that land of bondage a new nation under divine leadership, so now believers in Christ, having been born of God, are constituted a new nation whose citizenship is in Heaven. These Christian believers, though living in this world, are not of it nor to be fashioned according to it. Their habits and motives are of an altogether different order to what once characterized them as walking according to the flesh.

A New Nation (1 Peter 2:1-10)

Separation from the world and its influences was symbolically emphasized in God's command to the Israelites during the Passover. They were commanded to put away all leaven out of their houses and eat only unleavened bread with the bitter herbs and the roasted lamb (Exodus 12:8-15). In 1 Corinthians 5:7-8 we read:

> Purge out therefore the old leaven, that ye may be a new lump, as ye are unleavened. For even Christ our Passover is sacrificed for us: Therefore let us keep the feast, not with old leaven, neither with the leaven of malice and wickedness; but with the unleavened bread of sincerity and truth.

This is what Peter exhorted the believers in the beginning of chapter 2.

One of our hymns says:

> Lord, since we sing as pilgrims,
> Oh, give us pilgrim ways;
> Low thoughts of self, befitting
> Proclaimers of Thy praise.
> Oh, make us each more holy,
> In spirit pure and meek,
> More like to heavenly citizens
> As more of heaven we speak.

We are admonished to lay "aside all malice, and all guile, and hypocrisies, and envies, and all evil speakings" (2:1). What a clearing out of the old corrupt leaven is suggested here! How tightly these things cling to us even after we have been saved! With what readiness do we yield to the dictates of the old nature, giving way to unholy feelings, engendering ill feelings, and forgetting we are to speak evil of no man. A thorough searching of our hearts for leaven such as these words describe, and burning it in the fire of self-judgment is most important as we begin the heavenward journey.

In order to obtain strength for the Christian life we need nourishment, and that of a divine order. So just as newborn babes desire milk we should thirst for the genuine milk of the Word, the revealed truth of God. The Revised version adds "that by it you may grow unto salvation." This does not mean in order to obtain salvation in the sense of deliverance from the guilt of sin, but that salvation which means complete conformity to Christ to which we will never attain until we see Him as He is. In the meantime, the more we meditate upon the Word the more like Christ we shall become, provided of course we have tasted already that the Lord is gracious. If we do not yet know Him we have not taken the first step in the pilgrim way.

Peter's two letters were based on two high and precious experiences in his life, which he was never able to forget. The first Epistle links definitely with that confession of Christ as the Son of the living God which Peter made in the coasts of Caesarea Philippi when Jesus declared, "Blessed art thou, Simon Barjona: for flesh and blood hath not revealed it unto thee, but my Father which is in heaven. And I say also unto thee, That thou art Peter [a stone], and upon this rock I will build my church; and the gates of hell shall not prevail against it" (Matthew 16:17-18). The second Epistle is linked just as definitely with the glorious vision on the mount of transfiguration, as we shall see when we come to consider it.

Whatever man may think, and however theologians may wrangle about the meaning of the Lord's words to Peter regarding the rock on which the church is built, there can be no room for doubt as to how Peter himself understood them. He wrote, "To whom [referring to the Lord of whose grace he had just spoken] coming, as unto a living stone, disallowed indeed of men, but chosen of God, and precious, Ye also, as lively stones, are built up a spiritual house" (2:4-5a). The house is the church. The Rock upon which it is built is Christ Himself, the living Stone. Every believer is also a living stone (made such by grace), built on Christ and cemented to his fellow-members by the Holy Spirit.

> View the vast building; see it rise.
> The work how great; the plan how wise!
> Nor can that faith be overthrown
> Which rests upon the living Stone.

The apostle Paul taught the same lesson in the closing verses of Ephesians 2.

But not only are believers viewed as stones built together for a habitation of God through the Spirit, we are also "an holy priesthood, to offer up spiritual sacrifices, acceptable to God by Jesus Christ" (1 Peter 2:5). How different is this teaching from Rome's claim to have authority to appoint a special priesthood who offer material sacrifices. They present a wafer before God and pretend it is changed into the body, blood, soul, and divinity of Jesus Christ, which is again immolated on their altars as a perpetual sacrifice for the sins of the living and the dead. The blasphemy of it all chills one's blood even as we pen the words!

In ancient Israel there were three special groups: the priesthood, the Levites, and the warriors. In the church, or assembly of God, all are priests to go unto God as worshipers; all are Levites to serve their brethren in holy things; all are soldiers to fight the good fight of faith. There is no separate priesthood now, no clerical order recognized by God as distinct from and with authority over those who are content to be called and call themselves mere laymen, or the laity.

All believers are a holy priesthood and a royal priesthood, as we learn in verse 9. We offer up "the sacrifice of praise...the fruit of our lips giving thanks to his name" (Hebrews 13:15). This was the real sacrifice, even in the days of types and shadows (Jeremiah 33:11).

Referring to the Rock foundation Peter quoted from Isaiah 28:16 where God declared, "Behold, I lay in Sion a chief corner stone, elect, precious: and he that believeth on him shall not be confounded." He who in God's eyes is the infinitely precious One is the elect Stone, the Head of the corner and the solid Rock on which the spiritual edifice is built. To those who believe in Him, He is indeed not only precious but also the preciousness; but unto the disobedient He is the rejected Stone whom God nevertheless has made Head of the corner (Psalm 118:22). Disowned by Israel and crucified, God raised Him from the dead and exalted Him to this high place. But despite all the many witnesses to His resurrection there are myriad who refuse to believe. They stumble at the Word because of their disobedience, and to this they are appointed. Do not misunderstand; they were not appointed or predestined to be disobedient. God does not so deal with any man. The supralapsarian theologians dishonor His name while imagining they are defending His right when they so teach. But when men are determined to go on in the path of disobedience, God gives them up to strong delusion, thus appointing them to stumble.

Believers are a chosen generation, not by physical birth, but by spiritual birth. They constitute a royal priesthood who, like Melchizedec, go out from the presence of God to bless mankind, and magnify the name of the Most High God. They are a holy nation, thus taking the place of that polluted nation which God has, for the time being, disowned. This new nation of pilgrims is now His peculiar people—that is, a people for His own possession—whose high calling it is to show forth the praises of Him who has called them out of the darkness of nature, of sin, and of unbelief, into the marvelous light and liberty of the gospel.

In time past, as Hosea predicted, they were not a people; now they are recognized by God as His own. They who were once *Lo-ruhamah* ("not having obtained mercy") now have obtained mercy through faith in Christ Jesus the Lord (Hosea 2:23).

The Pilgrim Character (1 Peter 2:11-25)

The Spirit of God now gives us important details concerning what should characterize the pilgrim band as they travel on through the wilderness of this world to the Canaan rest that awaits them. Let us notice carefully each verse.

"As strangers and pilgrims" (11). Note the order. Men often reverse it. But no one is really a pilgrim in this Biblical sense who has not first become a stranger in this world. As such, he is to be careful to avoid contamination with the evil that is all about him. He is to "abstain from fleshly lusts, which war against the soul." Just as Amalek came out and fought against Israel (Exodus 17:8), so these carnal desires would tend to turn the believer aside from the path of devotion to Christ, and so hinder his progress as he journeys on toward that which God has prepared for him (1 Peter 1:3-4).

"They may by your good works...glorify God" (2:12). Daniel's enemies had to confess they could find nothing against him except "concerning the law of his God," which was contrary to their accepted heathen practices (Daniel 6:4-5). In the same way, consistent believers shut the mouths of those who would deride and vilify them, making these very foes of the truth bear testimony to the consistency of their lives.

"Submit yourselves to every ordinance of man for the Lord's sake" (2:13). As loyal subjects of the state, Christians are to be obedient to the laws passed, even though they may feel that in some instances they are unnecessarily arbitrary and even actually unjust. By their submission they honor Him whom they recognize as their Lord and Savior. Whatever form of government may prevail, so long as it is recognized as the constituted authority of the country, we are to be in subjection whether to a king or by whatever name the supreme executive is known.

"Unto governors...for the punishment of evildoers" (14). Human government has been established by God that evil may be checked and righteousness encouraged. The fact that some rulers act contrary to the divine ideal does not absolve the believer from obedience to the powers that be. All human government manifests imperfection, but without its restraints society would be shipwrecked and anarchy would prevail. In principle, all constituted authority is intended to prevent crime and encourage honesty and good living.

"With well doing ye may put to silence the ignorance of foolish men" (15). Nothing is a better answer to false and malignant accusations than a godly, upright life against which no charges can be brought truthfully. Samuel was a good example of this (1 Samuel 12:3-4). There have always been evilly-disposed men who have sought to impugn the motives and malign the conduct of God-fearing people. The best answer to all this is a blameless life, and this involves obedience to law.

"As free, and not using your liberty for a cloak of maliciousness" (2:16). Christians have been called unto liberty (Galatians 5:13), but this must never be confused with license to obey the dictates of the flesh. He who makes of his Christian profession a cloak to cover unrighteous behavior is a hypocrite who dishonors the worthy name of the One he professes to serve. Note the vivid contrast in 2:16. Those who, through grace, are free from the slavery of sin and free from the principle of legality in Christian service are nevertheless the bondmen of God. They have been purchased with the precious blood of Christ, and so responsible to render glad, loving obedience to His Word. They are not to make their liberty an excuse for fleshly license.

There are four admonitions in verse 17. The third really covers all the rest. He who fears—that is, stands in awe of—God will not dishonor any man, and will love his brethren, and give due recognition to constituted authority. "Honour all men." No man is to be despised. All are among those for whom Christ died. "Love the brotherhood." This refers, not to the world in general, but to those who have been saved out of the world—those born again into the family of God. "Fear God." Reverence Him whom we now know, not only as Creator, but also as Redeemer. "Honour the king." Show due respect to the head of the government as one set by God in that very place, who is therefore accountable to God for the right exercise of the authority committed to him.

Servants are exhorted to obedience to their own masters, and that "not only to the good and gentle, but also to the froward" (18). It is easy to obey a master who is kindly disposed and considerate. But the grace of God is seen in yielding obedience to those who are harsh and needlessly severe. This verse has added force when we remember that in Peter's day servants were generally slaves. The consistent behavior of Christians in bondage was used of God to lead many of their masters to Christ. Self-vindication is ever to be avoided on the part of the follower of Christ. He is called to imitate his Master, who endured uncomplainingly the false accusation of sinners and lived His pure and holy life as under the eye of the Father, content to leave it with Him to justify Him in due time (Isaiah 50:5-8). The believer is to be subject to the laws of the land wherein he dwells, and to be a loyal citizen and an obedient servant in his particular calling. Thus by his good behavior he will show the falsity of the charges of malicious men who would seek to make him out a menace to the state and an enemy of mankind. The early Christians were often so charged, but their consistent lives silenced their accusers.

"This is thankworthy" (2:19). The real theme of Peter's first letter is the grace of God as revealed to and in the saints (5:12). The word rendered "thankworthy" here is really "grace." It is grace active in the life, enabling one to bear up under false accusations and to suffer in silence when conscious of one's own integrity.

"If, when ye do well, and suffer for it,...this is acceptable with God" (2:20). Anyone can endure reproof when he knows it is deserved. It takes grace to enable one to accept undeserved blame without complaining; but to God it is acceptable, or commendable, for this is to follow Christ's example. "It is hard to be blamed for what you did not do!" So said a troubled young Christian. But in this portion of God's Word we are exhorted to take our blessed, adorable Lord Himself as our example in this as in all else. He was falsely accused and bitterly persecuted for wrongs He had never done. As He left everything in the Father's hands, so should we. Nature will rebel when we have to say, as He did, "They laid to my charge things that I knew not" (Psalm 35:11). But grace will enable us to triumph and rejoice when men speak evil of us and persecute us (Matthew 5:11). If we endure patiently, as seeing Him who is invisible (Hebrews 11:27), we shall be vindicated in His own way and time, and reward will be sure at His judgment seat (1 Corinthians 4:5).

"Christ also suffered for us, leaving us an example" (2:21). He has trodden the path ahead of us. We are called to follow His steps. The word here rendered "example" suggests a top line in a child's copybook. We are to reproduce Christ in our lives.

"Who did no sin, neither was guile found in his mouth" (22). He was pure outwardly and inwardly, God's unblemished, spotless Lamb. Therefore He was a suitable sacrifice on behalf of sinners, as He would not have been had He Himself been in any way defiled.

"When he was reviled, reviled not again" (23). Jesus endured patiently all the shame and indignities to which wicked men subjected Him. Their evil accusations brought no answers from His holy lips. He left it to the Father to vindicate Him, in His own good time.

"Who his own self bare our sins in his own body on the tree" (24). We dislike being blamed for other people's faults, but He took all our sins upon Himself. He bore all the judgment due to us, and so we are healed by His stripes as depicted in Isaiah 53:5-6. Shall we then live in the sins for which He died? Rather, let us live now "unto righteousness" that He may be glorified in us.

"The Shepherd and Bishop of your souls" (2:25). Once we were all like straying sheep, but through the grace of God we have been brought to know Christ. He is now our Shepherd, feeding and sustaining us, and our Bishop, or Overseer, guiding and directing us as we pursue our onward way through the wilderness of this world.

Having been saved by Him whom the world rejected, His pilgrim people have no reason to expect better treatment from that world than what was meted out to their Lord. When incarnate Love was here on earth, few received Him and many rejected Him. His followers need not be surprised therefore if their testimony is spurned by the majority and accepted by the minority. The Christian is not to think it strange when he and that for which he stands are not highly esteemed by the world. He is here as a light to shine for Christ in a dark world. When Jesus our Lord returns He will estimate aright all that His people have done and suffered for His sake, and He will reward accordingly. In the meantime it is better far to have the approval of the Lord than the approbation of the world which crucified Him.

We may summarize the conduct that is taught in 1 Peter 2 as follows:

> purity of life (11)
> honesty in word and deed (12)
> subjection to law (13-15)
> walking in liberty, not license (16)
> reverence for God and consideration for men (17)
> obedience to masters (18)
> enduring grief (19)
> patient under false accusations (20)
> following Christ's footsteps (21-23)
> dead to sins and living unto righteousness (24)
> acknowledging Christ's authority, and submitting to His
>   care (25)

These are the characteristics of the new life that we who are saved have received by our second birth.

CHAPTER THREE
THE PILGRIMS' UNITY

T he new life does not run counter to natural relationships. It is no sign of grace but rather quite the opposite to be without natural affection. So the Holy Spirit now proceeds to admonish wives and husbands as to their attitude toward each other.

The Christian Family (1 Peter 3:1-7)

There are few experiences more difficult than to be united in marriage to an unbeliever. The Christian young man or young woman should never go voluntarily into such a union. "Be ye not unequally yoked together with unbelievers...what communion hath light with darkness?...or what part hath he that believeth with an infidel?" (2 Corinthians 6:14-15). But where one member of a family already formed comes to know the Lord while the other remains in the darkness of nature, the most serious misunderstandings and perplexing circumstances are apt to arise. If it be the wife who has been converted while the husband remains out of Christ, special wisdom and grace will be needed on her part. If she takes a superior attitude toward her unsaved husband she will only stir up his opposition to the truth and render conditions increasingly difficult. She is admonished here to be in subjection to her own husband, exhibiting such grace and humility of spirit that even though he resents the Word he may be won without the word—that is, without the wife saying much to him (3:1). He may be persuaded by her discreet behavior as he observes the beauty of her Christian character. We say that

83

"actions speak louder than words," and this is in accord with the teaching of Scripture. An imperious, dominating woman will drive her husband further from God instead of drawing him to Christ. But a gentle, gracious lady, whose life is characterized by purity and whose adorning is not simply that which is outward but that which is inward, will have great influence over even a godless husband.

Here let me point out that the Scriptures do not forbid a measure of adornment of the person, but rather that the wife should not depend on this to make her pleasing and attractive. A slovenly woman only repels. But one may be tastefully attired and immaculately groomed, and yet spoil everything by a haughty spirit or a bad temper. The "ornament of a meek and quiet spirit" is in God's sight priceless, and will commend the woman who possess it to her husband, family, and friends (4).

It was in this way that the holy women of the Old Testament were adorned. They lived in dependence on God and were in subjection to their husbands instead of domineering over them. Sarah is cited as a beautiful example of this (6). When the angel announced that she was to become the mother of Isaac, though at a very advanced age, she wonderingly inquired how it could be when she was old. She added, "My lord being old also," referring to her husband Abraham in respectful, submissive terms (Genesis 18:12). Those who obey the instruction of 1 Peter 3:1-5 exhibit that they are Sarah's children morally, and need not be terrified by trying and difficult experiences.

To the husbands there is also a word of serious admonition (7): Let him give all due honor to his wife, not trying to lord his authority over her conscience. Recognizing her physical limitations as the weaker vessel, let him be the more considerate, dwelling with her according to knowledge and as being heirs together of the grace of life. And the Spirit added what is most important: "That your prayers be not hindered." Quarrels and bickerings in the home stifle all fellowship in prayer. It means much for the husband and wife to be able to kneel together in hallowed communion and mingle their voices in prayer and intercession.

Suffering for Righteousness' Sake (1 Peter 3:8-22)

Verse 8 begins with the word "Finally," which suggests that what follows is not to be divorced from what has gone before but rather is the natural result of it. Believers generally, not only husbands and wives, now are exhorted to evidence oneness of spirit, sympathetic consideration for each other with brotherly love, the product of a gracious heart and a lowly mind. Anything like retaliation for injuries is to be sedulously avoided. In place of returning evil for evil and reviling for reviling we are to bless even our worst opponents, for in so doing we ourselves will be doubly blessed (9).

Peter quoted a part of the thirty-fourth Psalm, using verses 12-16, but he stopped in the middle of the last sentence, and that for a very special reason. The Psalmist addressed all who love life and would enjoy it at its best, admonishing them to keep their tongues from evil and their lips from speaking guile—that is, anything of a dishonest character. He exhorted them to turn from evil unto righteousness, to seek peace and pursue it—that is, ever follow after that which is for the good of mankind. And all this is in view of the fact that the all-seeing eyes of Jehovah are upon the righteous, and His ears are open to their prayers; but the face of the Lord is against them that do evil. There Peter stopped. When we turn back to Psalm 34 we find verse 16 continues, "To cut off the remembrance of them from the earth." But that will not be in this age. It will have its solemn fulfillment in the coming day of the Lord. So exact and meticulous is Scripture! We might think that it made little difference, but Jesus put a whole dispensation into a comma when He read from Isaiah in the synagogue at Nazareth, "He hath anointed me...to preach the acceptable year of the Lord. And he closed the book" (Luke 4:18-20). The next words in Isaiah are, "and the day of vengeance of our God" (61:2); but that day will not begin until the day of grace is ended.

No matter how evil men motivated by Satanic hatred for the gospel may seek to injure believers, "who is he that will harm you, if ye be followers of that which is good?" (1 Peter 3:13) There can no evil happen to the righteous for, "all things work together for good to them that love God, to them who are the called according to his purpose" (Romans 8:28) . This includes persecution, sickness, financial distress—anything that men think of as evil, but all of which God sanctifies to the good of the obedient Christian.

If called upon to suffer for righteousness' sake let it be counted a joyful privilege (3:14). There is no need to fear nor to live in dread of threatened terror, for God is over all and none can go beyond that which He permits for our blessing. He who stopped the lions' mouths and protected Daniel, and walked in the furnace with the three Hebrew youths will ever keep a watchful eye upon His saints, and upon their enemies too, lest they go beyond His permissive will.

Only give God His rightful place in the heart. Let it be separated to Him, and when called to witness before men be ever ready to give an answer to all who inquire concerning the basis of your faith, with becoming humility and reverence (15). Be careful to maintain a good conscience so that there will be no truth to the charges of wicked men who give false testimony regarding your upright manner of life in Christ.

Verse 17 declares that it is better—that is, preferable—if it pleases God to allow it, that one suffer for doing right rather than for doing what is wrong. In this our blessed Lord is our supreme example. He suffered at the hands of evil men who misrepresented Him and bore false witness concerning Him. Then on the cross He suffered once for all for sins—not His own but ours—He the Just, we the unjust, in order that He might bring us to God. And this He has done. We have not yet been brought to Heaven, but we who believe in Christ Jesus have been brought to God.

On the cross He was put to death in the flesh, but in God's due time He was made alive by the Holy Spirit in His physical resurrection from the dead. Observe, it is not His human spirit that is here in view. It could not properly be said that He was quickened or made alive in His human spirit, for His spirit never died. But after the body and spirit had been separated in death He was raised again by the Holy Spirit (see Romans 8:11).

In that same Spirit He, in ages long gone by, preached through Noah to spirits with whom He declared He would not strive for more than an hundred and twenty years (Genesis 6:3). Noah was a preacher of righteousness and suffered for righteousness' sake, as we are called to do and as Jesus did (2 Peter 2:5). So it was "when once the longsuffering of God waited in the days of Noah, while the ark was a preparing," that Christ by the Spirit preached in or through that patriarch. What was the result of this preaching? "Wherein few, that is, eight souls were saved by water" (1 Peter 3:20). And just as those who entered the ark passed through the flood of judgment to a new earth, so in baptism the obedient believer is saved in symbol (21). It is not the going into the water that saves but we are saved by that which baptism represents and which a good conscience demands: the resurrection of Jesus Christ from the dead. He who went down into death, who could say, "All thy waves and thy billows are gone over me" (Psalm 42:7), has now emerged in triumph, bringing over to new creation all who trust in Him. He has gone into Heaven and sits as the exalted Son on the right hand of God, in token of the Father's full satisfaction in the work of His Son. To Him all angels, authorities, and powers are subject.

CHAPTER FOUR

THE PILGRIM'S SUFFERING

Conversion to God involves an inward and an outward change. When born again one receives a new nature with new desires and new ambitions. The whole behavior is changed from that of a selfish worldling to a devoted follower of the Lord Jesus Christ. The great importance of this is emphasized in the opening verses of 1 Peter 4.

The New Life Contrasted with the Old (1 Peter 4:1-11)

With Christ Himself as our example of patience in suffering how can we, who owe all to Him, do otherwise than arm ourselves with the same mind and so endure as beholding Him by faith? Many times God uses suffering to keep us from going into that which would dishonor Him. And when exposed to severe temptation it is as we suffer in the flesh that we are kept from sin. In this we may see the difference between our Lord's temptations and those which we have to face. He was tempted in all points like as we, apart from sin. He did not have a sinful nature as we do. He was from His birth the holy One. He could say, "The prince of this world cometh and hath nothing in me" (John 14:30). With us it is otherwise. When Satan attacks from without there is an enemy within—sin, the flesh— that responds to his appeal. It is only as we reckon ourselves dead to sin but alive unto God that we are enabled to mortify the deeds of the body. This often means suffering of a very severe character. But we are told, Jesus "suffered being tempted" (Hebrews 2:18). So infinitely pure and holy was He that it caused Him intense suffering even to be exposed to Satan's solicitations. He overcame by the Word of God, and the devil left Him for a season, to return in the hour of His agony as He was bearing our sins upon the cross.

Let us therefore resist every temptation to gratify the flesh, cost what it may, for it is our new responsibility to live no longer in the flesh according to carnal desires, but in the Spirit to the glory of God. A careful consideration of Galatians 5 will help to make clear what Peter presented to us as to our responsibility to refrain from ways that once characterized us. In their unsaved days those whom Peter addressed followed the ways of the Gentiles when they associated with the ungodly in lasciviousness, lusts, excess of wine, reveling, banqueting, and the abominations connected with idolatry. The Jews sought to curry favor with their pagan Gentile neighbors by participation in these evil things, even as Israel had done at Baal-Peor (Numbers 25:1-3) . Since their conversion to God all this was changed. Their former companions could not understand why they so suddenly and completely turned from lives of self-indulgence to what seemed to them great self-denial and austerity. They who applauded them before, now spoke evil of them. But Christians are to live as those who should give account not to men, but to Him who is about to judge the living and the dead when He returns in power. In that day those who despised them for their holy lives will answer to God too.

"For this cause was the gospel preached also to them that are dead, that they might be judged according to men in the flesh, but live according to God in the spirit" (4:6). Those who had preceded them in the path of faith were obliged to contend with similar conditions. For when the good news was preached to them they had to face the ridicule and even persecution of wicked men who had no understanding of spiritual things. Though their predecessors in the faith were now dead, this gospel was revealed to them so that even while living in this world and judged by their fellows as fools and fanatics, they might actually live unto God in spirit. There is no thought or suggestion here of the gospel being carried to men after death as Romanists, Mormons, and others would have us believe.

The Christian is ever to keep the end in view (7). He is to live not for the passing moment, but as one who knows that the end of all things—that is, all things of this present order—is at hand. It will be ushered in at the Lord's return; therefore, the importance of sobriety and watchfulness unto prayer.

Verse 8 emphasizes that which Paul stressed in 1 Corinthians 13, the importance of fervent love among those who are of the pilgrim company. The world hates believers. This is all the more reason why they cling to one another in love, even though they cannot be blind to the faults of others. But love covers the multitude of sins, rather than exposing and holding them up to censure. This does not mean that we should be indifferent to evil. We are taught elsewhere how to deal with and to help those who are overtaken in a fault or who drift into sin. See Galatians 6:1; James 5:19-20.

It is incumbent on those who love Christ to be gracious to one another, using hospitality ungrudgingly, as verse 9 tells us.

Verses 10 and 11 have to do with the exercise of spiritual gifts and Christian service generally. Each person is responsible to use the gift he has received to minister for the blessing of the rest, "as good stewards of the manifold grace of God." A steward is held accountable to fulfill faithfully the trust committed to him by his master.

They who speak, addressing the church when assembled together, are not to give out their own or other men's theories. They are to speak as the oracles of God, declaring only that which He has revealed. Those who minister or serve in any capacity are to do it according to the ability God gives, so that in all things He may be glorified through Christ Jesus to whom all praise and dominion eternally belong.

Suffering as a Christian (1 Peter 4:12-19)

The name *Christian* is not found very often in the New Testament, but is the distinctive title of those who belong to Christ. We read of it in Acts 11:26 where it was conferred upon the Gentile believers at Antioch by divine authority; for the word *called* there literally means "oracularly called," and therefore it was not the Antiochians alone who bestowed this name upon the believers, but God Himself who so designated them. That it had become their well-known appellation is evident from Acts 26:28 where we read that King Agrippa exclaimed, "Almost thou persuadest me to be a Christian." When Peter wrote his first letter some years later he used it as the commonly recognized name of the pilgrim company, and he explained that it is praiseworthy to suffer as a Christian.

In verse 12 we read of "the fiery trial which is to try you." Primarily, the reference was to the great suffering that the Jews—whether Christian or not—were about to undergo in connection with the fulfillment of our Lord's prophecy concerning Jerusalem's destruction, shortly to take place (Luke 21:20-24). But "the fiery trial" also has reference to the horrors of the Roman persecutions, which were to continue for two terrible centuries. The words are applicable to every time of trial and persecution.

"Partakers of Christ's sufferings" (4:13). The believer suffers in fellowship with his Lord. Our Lord has told us to expect this (John 15:18-21). We cannot be partakers of His atoning sufferings. They stand alone: none but He could endure the penalty for our sins and so make propitiation in order that we might be forgiven. But we share His sufferings for righteousness' sake.

"Reproached for the name of Christ" (4:14). No one can be true to Christ and loved by the world system, for everything that Jesus taught condemns the present order and leads ungodly men to hate Him and His people. But he who suffers for Christ's sake now is assured of glory hereafter, which will fully answer to the shame now endured. "On their part he is evil spoken of, but on your part he is glorified." The reproach of the world should not deter the Christian. He need not expect the approval of those who reject and misunderstand his Savior. It is his responsibility to live so as to prove false the derogatory reports of the ungodly and so to glorify the One whose name they spurn.

No believer should ever suffer as "a busybody in other men's matters" (15). Notice the company in which the busybody is placed. He is linked with murderers, thieves, and evildoers of every description, and that for a very good reason; for the busybody steals men's reputations, seeks to assassinate their good names, and by his calumniations works all manner of evil. The follower of Christ is exhorted to be careful never to misbehave so as to deserve the ill-will of the wicked. He is not to be dishonest or corrupt in life, nor to be given to gossipy interference in other people's affairs. Thus by a holy and righteous life he will adorn the gospel of Christ (Philippians 1:27-28).

"If any man suffer as a Christian, let him not be ashamed" (4:16). No one needs to be ashamed to suffer because of his faithfulness to the holy name he bears. The disciples, as we have noticed already, were called Christians first at Antioch, and this name has clung to them ever since. It signifies their union with Christ, and therefore is a name in which to glory, however the world may despise it. Let us therefore never be ashamed of this name and all that it implies, but be prepared to suffer because of it, knowing that we may thus glorify the God who has drawn us to Himself and saves us through His blessed Son, who bore our sins in His own body on the tree (1 Peter 2:24).

"Judgment must begin at the house of God" (4:17). Our Father-God does not pass over the failures of His people, but disciplines them in order that they may be careful to walk in obedience to His Word. If He is so particular in chastening His own, how solemn will be the judgment of "them that obey not the gospel," but persist to the end in rejecting the Savior He has provided!

"If the righteous scarcely be saved"—that is, if the righteous have to endure chastening at the hand of God and persecution at the hand of the world—what will it mean for unsaved and impenitent men to answer before the judgment throne for their persistence in refusing His grace? (18)

Christians are to "commit the keeping of their souls to him in well doing, as unto a faithful Creator" (19). However hard the way and however perplexing his experiences, the suffering Christian may look up to God in confidence. He is assured that he can rely on the divine love and faithfulness to work out all for blessing at last.

Throughout the entire Christian era, which is that of the dispensation of the grace of God (Ephesians 3:2), believers in Christ are called out from the world and are responsible to live for the glory of Him who has saved them. But though separated from the surrounding evil, they are not to shut themselves up as in a monastery or convent in order to be protected from defilement. They are to go forth as God's messengers into that very world from which they have been delivered, preaching to all men everywhere the gospel, which is God's offer of salvation through the finished work of His beloved Son. Whatever suffering or affliction this entails is to be borne cheerfully for His sake, knowing that when He returns in glory He will reward abundantly for all trials endured. His church is to be in the world, but not of it, witnessing against its evil and offering pardon through the cross.

Tertullian declared that the blood of the martyrs is the seed of the church. This has been demonstrated over and over again. Persecution can never destroy the church of God. The more it is called to suffer for Christ, the stronger it becomes. It is internal strife and carelessness in life that endangers it. But so virile is the life it possesses that even this has never been permitted to destroy it, for although its outward testimony has at times been ruined by such things, God has always kept alive a witnessing remnant to stand for the truth of His Word.

CHAPTER FIVE

THE PILGRIM'S GLORY

The path of suffering, both for Christ and for His followers, ends in glory. Peter has a special word for his fellow elders, to whom was committed the care of the flock of God, and who were specially exposed to the assaults of the enemy.

The End of the Way (1 Peter 5:1-4)

Note the expression, "the elders which are among you." There is no suggestion here of a clerical order ruling arbitrarily over the laity. These elders were mature, godly men on whom rested the responsibility of watching over the souls of believers, as those for whom they must give an account (Hebrews 13:17). Peter linked himself with them, "who am also an elder," or "who am a co-presbyter." If Peter was ever a pope he never knew it! He took his place as one with his elder-brethren in sharing the ministry for the edification of the saints, even though he was one of the original twelve, and so a witness of the sufferings of Christ. And he was yet to share in the glory that will be revealed at the Lord's second advent.

He admonished the elders to feed, not fleece, "the flock of God which is among you." They were to feed the people by ministering the truth of God as made known in His holy Word. What a grievous thing it is when men, professing to be servants of Christ, set before the sheep and lambs of His flock, unscriptural teachings which cannot edify but only mislead.

These elders were to take the oversight not as pressed unwillingly into a service which was a hard, unwelcome task. Nor were they to assume leadership for what money was to be gained thereby, but as serving the Lord with a willing mind. Neither were they to become ecclesiastical lords, dominating over God's heritage. Think of the hierarchy that has been developed in the professing body, with its priests, lord-bishops, cardinals known as "princes of the church," and all the other dignitaries who rule as with an iron hand those under their jurisdiction. Could anything be more opposed to what Peter teaches here? Yet some call him the first pope!

Whatever authority the elders have springs from lives of godliness and subjection to the Lord. They are to be examples whom the sheep of Christ may safely follow (3).

Their reward will be sure when they reach the end of the way and they will give account of their service to the chief Shepherd at His glorious appearing. His own blessed hands will bestow on each faithful under-shepherd an unfading victor's wreath of glory—the token of His pleasure in the service they have done as unto Him.

Grace Operative on the Journey (1 Peter 5:5-14)

We have seen that throughout this Epistle Peter emphasized the grace of God as that which enables the believer to triumph in all circumstances. He stressed this most definitely in the concluding section of this Epistle.

As we walk in obedience to Him who is meek and lowly in heart we can appreciate the preciousness of that grace which He gives to the humble. Pride is a barrier to all spiritual progress and should have no place in the Christian company. None should ever be puffed up against others. All are to be submissive to one another, not only the younger to the elder, as is befitting, but each to his brethren, and all clothed with humility. For God sets Himself against the proud and haughty, but ministers all needed grace to enable the meek to overcome, no matter what difficulties they are called to face.

"Humble yourselves therefore...that he may exalt you in due time" (6). We are to take the lowly place of unquestioning submission to the will of God now, knowing on the authority of His Word that in the day of His revealing He will note all we have endured for His name's sake, and He will then give abundant reward.

"He careth for you" (7). It is of all importance to realize that God's heart is ever toward His own. He is no indifferent spectator of our suffering. He feels for us in our afflictions and bids us cast every care upon Him. We may rest assured that He is concerned about all we have to endure. Weymouth has rendered the last part of this verse, "It matters to God about you." How precious to realize this!

"Your adversary the devil...walketh about" (8). Satan is a real being, a malignant personality, the bitter enemy of God and man. But when we refuse to give place to the devil, standing firmly at the cross, he flees from us, and his power is broken. We are to stand against all the devil's suggestions, "stedfast in the faith," battling for the truth committed to us (9). Nor are we alone in this struggle: our brethren everywhere have the same enemy to face.

"After that ye have suffered a while" (10). We grow by suffering. Only thus can God's plan of conformity to Christ be carried out. But all is ordered of Him and He will not permit one trial too many. When His purpose is fulfilled we will be perfected and made strong in His grace.

"To Him be glory and dominion for ever and ever" (11). The victory will be His at last. All evil will be put down as Satan will be shut up in his eternal prison. Suffering then will be only a memory. God will be glorified in all His saints, and His dominion established over all the universe.

In verse 12 Peter mentioned the name of his amanuensis, Silvanus, whom Peter regarded as a faithful brother to them and to himself. He may be the same Silas, or Silvanus, who accompanied Paul on his second missionary journey; or he may have been another of the same, not uncommon, name. The theme of the entire Epistle is here declared to be "the true grace of God wherein ye stand." As intimated in our introduction, while these words are much like those of Paul in Romans 5:2—"This grace wherein we stand"—the meaning is different. Paul wrote of our standing in grace before God; Peter testified to the power of grace that enables us to stand in the hour of trial, neither giving place to the devil nor disheartened by suffering and persecution. There are abundant stores of grace from which we may draw freely for strength to meet every emergency as we pursue our pilgrim way.

This letter was written at Babylon, which Romanists claim was pagan Rome, but it seems more likely it was, as the Nestorian church has held from the beginning, Babylon on the Euphrates, where many Jews lived to whom Peter ministered. Another view, with apparently less evidence and held by the Coptic church, is that the city was a new Babylon in Egypt near to the present city of Cairo. Wherever it was, the church there joined Peter in salutations to the scattered Christians throughout Asia Minor. Mark also participated in this greeting. He is identical with the John Mark who was the companion for a time of Paul and Barnabas, and who, though unfaithful at first, became accredited later to Paul's own satisfaction (2 Timothy 4:11). According to some very early writers Mark accompanied Peter in later years and wrote his Gospel in collaboration with the venerable apostle, under the Holy Spirit's guidance.

The Epistle closes with a benediction quite different from those that bring Paul's letters to an end. Paul always wrote of grace: Peter directed the saints to greet one another with a kiss of love, and prayed that peace may be with all that are "in Christ Jesus." These three final words are significant. We ordinarily think of them as characteristic of Paul's writings. He used the expressions "in Christ" and "in Christ Jesus" with great frequency. Peter joined with Paul in speaking of the saints in this blessed relationship. They are no longer in the flesh or in Adam; they are new by new birth and the gift of the indwelling Spirit in Christ Jesus, and so a new creation.

SECOND PETER

SECOND PETER
FACING THE END

BY JOHN PHILLIPS

Controversy has raged around the authorship of 2 Peter, but despite the difference of tone between 2 Peter and 1 Peter, there are still good reasons for holding to the view that both letters were written by Peter. There is , of course, the direct claim of 2 Peter to be from Peter (1:1). The writer claims to be an apostle (1:1), claims to have been on the mount of transfiguration (1:16-18), claims to have been told by the Lord that he would die (1:13-15; John 21:18-19); and knew of Paul's Epistles (3:15-16). Moreover there is a close resemblance between the two Epistles, and the writer of 2 Peter claims to have written to his readers before (3:1).

In his second letter Peter continued the practical teaching so characteristic of his first one, and he goes on to speak forcefully of the Lord's second coming. Peter knew he was soon to die. It is presumed that the second Epistle was written not long after the first, probably before the fall of Jerusalem in A.D. 70. Peter's martyrdom took place about A.D. 68. Second Peter and Second Timothy have much in common, both writers being aware that martyrdom was near (2 Timothy 4:6; 2 Peter 1:14). Both warn of apostasy and both reflect the joyful spirit of the writers.

Although Paul and Jude had written warning letters against the heretical teachings then making drastic inroads into the church, Peter felt he must fling the weight of his own personal authority and influence onto the scales. Peter enjoyed a tremendous reputation in the early church and a vast fund of goodwill. So with the shadows lengthening as the first century of the Christian era moved into its second half, Peter wrote. And some of the insights he had are astonishing indeed. He even foresaw the dawning of the nuclear age as a herald of the great and terrible "day of the Lord."

Second Peter deals with faith's conviction, contention, and consummation.

I. FAITH'S CONVICTION (1:1-21)
   A. As to the Walk with God (1:1-15)
      1. The Secret of Commencing Well (1:1-4)
         a. How to Be Saved (1:1-3a)
         b. How to Be Sure (1:3b-4a)
         c. How to Be Sanctified (1:4b)
      2. The Secret of Continuing Well (1:5-9)
         a. The Path of Diligence (1:5-8)
            (1) Faithful Addition (1:5-7)
            (2) Fruitful Abundance (1:8)
         b. The Path of Delusion (1:9)
      3. The Secret of Concluding Well (1:10-15)
         a. Peter's Exhortation (1:10-12)
            (1) The Nature of It (1:10-11)
            (2) The Need for It (1:12)
         b. Peter's Example (1:13-15)
            (1) His Unfaltering Determination (1:13)
            (2) His Unforgettable Destiny (1:14)
            (3) His Unfailing Diligence (1:15)
   B. As to the Word of God (1:16-21)
      1. Its Integrity (1:16a)
      2. Its Instruction (1:16b-18)
      3. Its Importance (1:19a)
      4. Its Illumination (1:19b)
      5. Its Interpretation (1:20)
      6. Its Inspiration (1:21)
II. FAITH'S CONTENTION (2:1-22)
   A. The Doctrine of the Heretics (2:1-3a)
      1. Their Lying Message (2:1)

a. It Was Deceitful (2:1a)
b. It Was Damnable (2:1b)
2. Their Loose Morals (2:2)
3. Their Low Motive (2:3a)
B. The Doom of the Heretics (2:3b-9)
1. Its Nearness (2:3b)
2. Its Nature (2:4-9)
a. An Appeal in View of Past History (2:4-8)
(1) The Flood in Noah's Day (2:4-5)
(a) The Sinning Angels (2:4)
(b) The Sinning Antediluvians (2:5)
(2) The Fire in Lot's Day (2:6-8)
b. An Application in View of Present Heresy (2:9)
C. The Deeds of the Heretics (2:10-22)
1. An Exposure of Their Conduct (2:10-14)
a. Its Brazenness (2:10-12)
b. Its Boldness (2:13-14)
2. An Exposure of Their Claims (2:15-19)
a. A Biblical Sketch (2:15-16)
b. A Biographical Sketch (2:17-19)
(1) Their Empty Profession (2:17)
(2) Their Empty Preaching (2:18)
(3) Their Empty Promises (2:19)
3. An Exposure of Their Converts (2:20-22)
a. The Truth Revealed to Them (2:20)
b. The Truth Rejected by Them (2:21)
c. The Truth Related about Them (2:22)
III. FAITH'S CONSUMMATION (3:1-18)
A. Peter Exposes the Scoffers (3:1-13)
1. The Insistent Denial of the Promise of the Lord's
Return (3:1-4)
a. Why This Denial Would Be (3:1-2)
b. When This Denial Would Be (3:3)
c. What This Denial Would Be (3:4)
2. Their Ignorant Denial of the Promise of the Lord's
Return (3:5-13)

Their Ignorance of:
a. The Lord's Past Dealings with the Heaven and Earth—His Wrath Experienced (3:5-6)
b. The Lord's Present Dealings with the Heaven and Earth—His Wrath Expected (3:7-12)
   (1) The Truth of This (3:7)
   (2) The Time of This (3:8-9)
   (3) The Terror of This (3:10-12)
c. The Lord's Predicted Dealings with the Heaven and Earth—His Wrath Exhausted (3:13)
B. Peter Exhorts the Saints (3:14-18)
   1. To Behave (3:14)
   2. To Believe (3:15-16)
   3. To Beware (3:17-18)

As we read 2 Peter we must remember Nero was still on the rampage, that apostasy was taking swift root, and that Peter was soon to die—and he knew it.

It is one thing to start well in the Christian faith; it is something else to finish well. That was Peter's burden in the first chapter. Having reminded the saints that they had become "partakers of the divine nature," he went on to show that the Christian life thereafter was largely a matter of addition (1:5-7). Peter coveted for believers an abundant entrance into the everlasting kingdom (1:11) and cited himself as an example of one who, with but a short time to live, was still faithful in serving his Lord. He urged the saints to rest their faith squarely on the Word of God.

Chapter 2 is devoted to an exposure of heresy, which was already making its inroads into the assemblies of God's people. Peter reminded his readers that heresies were not something new; they had characterized the Old Testament era and had been duly punished by God. The error against which Peter warned was accompanied by immoral tendencies, pride, and covetousness, and would certainly meet with the judgment of God.

Finally, Peter reminded his readers that the last days would see the coming of a generation of scoffers mocking advent truth. The patience of God and His longsuffering would, however, one day be exhausted and a fearful catastrophe of fire would overtake the globe.

Peter's remarkable prophecy concerning the day of the Lord (3:10-11) is well worth careful study. The words he used are most accurate and descriptive. The word "elements" is a translation of the Greek word *stoicheia*, which carries the meaning of the letters of the alphabet. Greek scholars such as Liddell and Scott tell us that it conveys the thought of "the components into which matter is ultimately divided." In modern language, the word would simply mean "atoms."

The word for "dissolved" literally means to break up, destroy, or melt. It is translated "unloose" in several places in the New Testament.

The phrase "a great noise" signifies, according to W. E. Vine, "with rushing sound as of roaring flames." The same authority tells us that "with fervent heat" signifies a fever. Peter's is the only known use of the expression in connection with inanimate objects.

Thus Peter, an ignorant and unlearned fisherman, under the inspiration of the Holy Spirit, has accurately described for us, in nontechnical language, something that has been reserved for the twentieth century to really appreciate. Many are convinced that the dawn of the atomic age has brought the world to the threshold of "that great and terrible day of the Lord" (Joel 2:31).

Peter's second Epistle is a timely one for today. Since God will one day make all things new, we are urged to live godly lives, giving heed to all the Scriptures.

INTRODUCTION

How much time elapsed between the writing of Peter's two Epistles we have no way of determining. But certainly when one says, "This second epistle...I now write unto you" (3:1), it implies that the first one had been sent on just a short time before. This was true in regard to Paul's two letters to the Corinthians, those to the Thessalonians, and the two pastoral letters to Timothy.

Paul was, in all probability, already with the Lord when Peter wrote, or else he was enduring his last imprisonment just prior to his martyrdom, for Peter mentioned "all his [Paul's] epistles" as being in circulation already (3:15-16). This is important, inasmuch as some have sought to minimize the importance of Peter's written ministry in order to enhance the value of Paul's letters. But God does not set one apostle against another in this way. All Scripture is divinely inspired, and all is profitable. And as Peter was led of God to write these letters possibly after Paul's ministry had come to a close we dare not underestimate their value. They contain precious and important truth that the church can neglect only at its peril.

It is true that in early days some sought to cast doubt on the authenticity of this second Epistle, but there can be no question now as to this. It bears every mark of inspiration and, as such, has been accepted by the church since the second century at least, and by many reliable witnesses from the time when it was first circulated, somewhere about A.D. 66 to 70.

Like all second Epistles it is corrective. In the first Epistles we hear the voice of the teacher. As a rule in second Epistles it is rather the prophet or the exhorter who speaks.

The theme of this letter is faithfulness in a day of apostasy. The three chapters form three distinct divisions.

I. THE BELIEVER'S BLESSINGS (2 Peter 1)
   A. Blessings Received and Growth in Grace (1-11)
   B. The Hope of the Coming Kingdom (12-21)
II. INCREASING APOSTASY (2 Peter 2)
   A. Lessons from the Past (1-9)
   B. Characteristics of Apostate Teachers (11-17)
   C. Forsaking the Truth to Follow False Philosophies (18-22)
III. LOOKING TO THE FUTURE (2 Peter 3)
   A. Dangers of Forgetting the Past and Denying the Future (1-7)
   B. The Day of the Lord and the Day of God (8-14)
   C. A Final Warning (15-18)

We should be very grateful to God that He has given such a faithful portrayal of conditions that He foresaw from the first, in order that we might not be disheartened when these things actually developed in the professing church.

THE BELIEVER'S BLESSINGS

A s we begin our consideration of this second Epistle it is well to remember that it was written as a final message from Christ's venerable servant, the apostle Peter. He wrote in view of his forthcoming martyrdom, in order to warn believers of the oncoming flood of error and apostasy that was to sweep over Christendom. This time of trial would necessitate real confidence in God and His Word on the part of those who were to be called on to face such disturbing conditions.

In a very blessed way the Spirit of God first puts before us the blessings that are ours as Christians, and the importance of growing in grace. As we grow in the knowledge of Christ we are given strength to stand against the evils threatening the church.

Blessings Received and Growth in Grace (2 Peter 1:1-11)

Peter addressed himself to the same scattered saints as mentioned in his first letter, but without indicating them according to the lands of their dispersion as before. But verse 1 of chapter 3 makes it clear that this second letter was sent to the same persons as the first one.

He simply wrote to them as those "that have obtained like precious faith with us through the righteousness of God and our Saviour Jesus Christ." Note the word *precious*, which we have seen is one of frequent occurrence in Peter's letters. He wrote of faith through the righteousness of God and our Savior Jesus Christ. This stands out in remarkable contrast to the theme so frequently emphasized by the apostle Paul—"the righteousness which is of God by faith" (Philippians 3:9). Paul's expression refers to the righteousness that God imputes to all who believe on the Lord Jesus Christ, who has met every demand of the throne of God regarding sin. But Peter emphasized an altogether different aspect of things: since Christ has died for all men, God in His righteousness has opened the door of faith to everyone who desires to enter. It would be unrighteous of God to refuse to save anyone who desired to avail himself of the result of the work of the cross. The very righteousness of God demands that faith be extended to all men.

This principle is the opposite of what some high Calvinists teach. They would have us believe that faith itself is a gift which God grants only to a limited number; that all men have not faith because it is not the will of God that they should have it. This is the very opposite of the teaching of the Holy Scriptures. God desires that all men should be saved and come to the knowledge of the truth. The reason that some men do not have faith is that they will not give heed to the Word, and "faith cometh by hearing, and hearing by the word of God" (Romans 10:17). Where men are ready and willing to hear, God can be depended upon to see that they obtain this precious gift of faith. It would be unrighteous in Him to do otherwise.

In the second verse we have again the apostolic salutation in which Peter prayed that grace and peace might be multiplied unto the believers through the full knowledge, or super-knowledge, of God and of Jesus Christ our Lord. This is a completeness of knowledge that only the Holy Spirit Himself can give. It is interesting to observe how frequently Peter used mathematical terms in both his Epistles. The word *multiplied*, for example, is also found in 1 Peter 1:2 where it is used in a similar connection. There is an abundance of grace and peace available for all who rest in simplicity of heart on the testimony God has given. His divine power has bequeathed to us everything that is necessary for spiritual life and piety. But this godly life can never be divorced from the knowledge of Him who has called us, not exactly *to* glory and virtue, but *by* His glories and virtues. In other words, it is as we become better acquainted with God revealed in Christ that we grow in grace and become more like Him with whom our souls are occupied.

In verse 1 the apostle wrote of *precious* faith; in verse 4 he reminded us that God has given us His surpassing great and *precious* promises. As we lay hold of these promises and dare to act on them we, who have been born again by believing the gospel, exhibit the divine nature in our practical lives. Thus we find deliverance from the corruption into which the whole world has been brought through lust—that is, through unlawful desire. The word *lust* should never be limited simply to fleshly concupiscence, but includes covetousness and every sort of yearning after that which God, in His infinite love and wisdom, has forbidden.

As we act upon the truth of the Word we will be prepared for that which follows in verses 5-7. Here again Peter wrote from a mathematical standpoint as he told us of the graces that should be *added* to our faith. A better figure perhaps is that of a growing tree: an acorn, for instance, falls into the ground; the seed germinates, strikes its roots downward, and its branches shoot upward, and that acorn becomes an entire oak tree with all its various parts. Faith is like the acorn—a living faith, that should characterize us as devoted Christians. So Peter said, "[Have in] your faith virtue." The virtue of which he speaks here is not simply chastity, as some might think, but it is really valor, which is the outstanding virtue of a soldier, and we are called to be soldiers of Christ. Then he added, "And [in] virtue knowledge." There can be no proper growth without a deepened understanding of spiritual realities. "[In] knowledge temperance," or self-control. A Christian who gives way to evil tempers, or careless habits of any kind, is not growing in self-control. "[In] temperance patience"—that which enables one to endure without complaining, even though exposed to circumstances that are very distasteful to the natural man. Peter continued, "[In] patience godliness," which is really "God-likeness," or true piety, as we have seen in considering the first Epistle. In godliness we will have brotherly kindness—consideration for all who, through the grace of God, belong to the Christian brotherhood. Last of all he added, "[In] brotherly kindness charity," or love. This is the full fruitage of faith, for Paul told us that faith expresses itself through love (Galatians 5:6).

If these qualities are found in a believer, and not in scanty measure but in abundance, the effect is to make him neither idle nor unfruitful in the knowledge of our Lord Jesus Christ. The King James version renders it, "Neither...barren nor unfruitful," but these terms are synonymous as ordinarily used. "Idle" or "inactive" is a better rendering of the original than the word *barren*. One who does not show these fruits of faith is designated here as blind, or myopic (9). He is unable to discern spiritual things. Though once truly born of God, he forgets the sins from which he has been purged and is likely to lapse into them again, thus coming under the discipline of God because of failure to go on with the Lord.

Peter concluded this exhortation in verses 10 and 11 by urging those to whom he wrote to "give diligence to make [their] calling and election sure"—that is, in the sense of giving evidence of their calling. No one has any reason to believe that one is numbered among the elect of God unless he is characterized by faith that produces fruit unto God. In a fruitful life there will be constant victory over tendencies toward evil, "For if ye do these things, ye shall never fall."

A promise is given that the final result will be a rich welcome into the everlasting kingdom of our Lord and Savior Jesus Christ. Observe, it is not an entrance into Heaven as such that is here put before us. Heaven is the Father's house, and to that all believers have exactly the same claim. It is the home of the Father's children, and the weakest and feeblest of saints will be as welcome there as the strongest and most useful. But the everlasting kingdom is another sphere: it speaks of reward, and our place in the kingdom is determined by our devotion to Christ in this world.

The Hope of the Coming Kingdom (2 Peter 1:12-21)

Next Peter referred to what the Lord had told him concerning his martyrdom. Jesus had made it very clear, in speaking to Peter on that morning by the seaside when He publicly restored him to the place of apostleship, that in his old age he would die for Christ's name's sake (John 21:18-19). Many years had passed since that memorable conversation, and Peter was now well advanced in years. He knew he could not remain much longer in this world, therefore he desired to leave behind a written ministry that the saints might be encouraged and established in the truth necessary for their present hour of testing.

Notice how he put it in verse 12, "Wherefore I will not be negligent to put you always in remembrance of these things, though ye know them, and be established in the present truth." He was not writing to young believers who were ignorant of the precious truths. But he knew the value of repetition because of the fact that we forget so easily. Therefore he considered it important as long as he remained in his fleshly tabernacle—that is, in his body—to stir up the saints by reminding them of these things. And he knew well that in a very short time he would be obliged to put off his fleshly tabernacle in accordance with what the Lord Jesus had revealed to him. Observe that he had no thought of going to sleep in his tabernacle as some modern materialists, masquerading under the Christian name, would have us believe. While alive on the earth Peter himself, the real man, lived in the body that he called his tabernacle; when death came he would move out of the tabernacle, and as Paul put it, go home "to be with Christ; which is far better" (Philippians 1:23). A comparison of this passage with 2 Corinthians 5:1-10 will prove most illuminating regarding the believer in life and in death. Scripture leaves no room whatever for the doctrine of the sleep of the soul, but only the sleep of the body until the Lord Jesus returns when the dead will be raised and the living changed (1 Thessalonians 4:15-17).

We have seen already that these two Epistles of Peter's were linked with two great experiences in his life during the earthly ministry of our blessed Lord. We have considered the first one in connection with the Lord's declaration as to the building of His church upon the truth that He was the Son of the living God (Matthew 16:15-18). In 2 Peter 1:15-18 Peter referred to that other great experience which took place on the mount of transfiguration (Matthew 17:1-8).

Guided by the Holy Spirit, Peter was unfolding truth that the Lord could use in after days for the comfort and sanctification of believers. He wrote of his own death as an exodus. The word translated "decease" is really the same as the title of the second book of the Old Testament. This agrees with what we have pointed out already:

At death Peter would be moving out from the body and going into the presence of the Lord. In view of the imminence of this event he endeavored to clarify certain truths that would enlighten the saints. He denied having followed cunningly devised fables when he and other inspired apostles had made known the power and the coming of the Lord Jesus Christ. They were eyewitnesses of His majesty when, on the mount of transfiguration, He was changed before them, and His inward glory shone out through the very clothing that He wore. Moses and Elijah appeared with Him at that time and spoke of His death that would take place at Jerusalem. When Peter suggested making three booths or tabernacles that they might linger there, a cloud covered the scene and a voice came from the excellent glory saying, "This is my beloved Son, in whom I am well pleased" (Matthew 17:5). This was not a dream, nor was it the effects of an excited imagination; but Peter said, "This voice which came from heaven we heard, when we were with him in the holy mount" (2 Peter 1:18). It was there that God granted to Peter, James, and John a view of the kingdom in miniature. They saw the Lord as He will yet be when He returns to reign in great power.

What they saw and heard on the mount confirmed the word of prophecy given in the Old Testament. Peter referred to the message of the prophets in the closing verses of the first chapter of this Epistle.

The opening clause of the nineteenth verse in the King James version seems to infer that Peter was telling us that the word of prophecy was even more sure than the Father's voice or the glory that the disciples saw; but that is not exactly what he says. This verse might better be read, "We have also the word of prophecy confirmed, and to this prophetic word believers do well to take heed in their hearts, for the lamp of prophecy is as a light that shineth in a dark place." It is intended by God to illumine our paths and give light in our souls until the day dawn, and the day star arise at the coming of our Lord Jesus Christ. It is all-important then that we give heed to that which has been revealed in the prophetic Scriptures. But on the other hand, we need to be careful lest we take some of these Scriptures out of their context and endeavor to interpret them according to specific incidents, rather than in accordance with the entire plan of God as revealed in His Word. No prophecy of the Scripture is of its own interpretation; none can be fully understood apart from the rest of Scripture.

Rome interprets this condemnation "of any private interpretation" as forbidding the individual believer to study the Word of God for himself and being guided by it directly, rather than through the interpretation given it by the church and its councils. But it is not that at all that Peter had in mind. Rather Peter wrote of the folly of taking some portion of the prophetic Word and endeavoring to apply it to some special circumstances, while failing to note its context and its connection with the general trend of prophecy as a whole. This is a snare to which many students of prophecy have been exposed, and numbers of them have failed at this very point. It means much to see that prophecy is one whole, and "known unto God are all his works from the beginning of the world" (Acts 15:18); and "the prophecy came not in old time by the will of man: but holy men of God spake as they were moved [or borne along] by the Holy Ghost" (2 Peter 1:21).

God has not desired to give in any Old Testament book a complete unfolding of the future concerning the glorious kingdom of Messiah and the events leading up to it. Yet by searching the writings of all the prophets and comparing Scripture with Scripture one is able to see, with at least a measure of clearness, the wonderful harmony of the prophetic Word. Also we will see the marvelous way in which God is unfolding the purpose of the ages when finally, in the dispensation of the fullness of times, Christ will reign as King of kings and Lord of lords.

CHAPTER TWO
INCREASING APOSTASY

The later Epistles of Paul and the Epistle of Jude bear witness to the fact that false doctrines had already begun to make serious inroads into the churches scattered throughout the world. Peter had this in mind when he wrote his final message to the saints. But he foresaw even greater apostasy in days to come, and so gave an inspired word of warning in order that the believers might not be carried away by the personality and persuasiveness of false teachers masquerading as servants of Christ.

The close connection between 2 Peter 2 and the Epistle of Jude has been noted often, and has given rise in some quarters to the idea that one is but a mutilated copy of the other. What we need to keep in mind is that the Holy Spirit Himself inspired both of these writers to portray conditions that the church of God would have to face in years to come. While Peter and Jude cover the same ground to some extent, there is one very striking difference between them: Peter emphasized the spread of unscriptural theories; whereas Jude emphasized the effects of these theories—turning the grace of God into lasciviousness. They give a twofold warning designed to save the elect of God from being misled. When once we realize that the Holy Spirit Himself is the author of all Scripture we will not be surprised to find that He speaks in similar terms through different servants; in fact, we should naturally expect this. "The testimony of two men is true," we are told; and by this double testimony God emphasizes those things that we need to keep in mind.

Lessons from the Past (2 Peter 2:1-9)

Peter turned our minds back to conditions that prevailed in former days, which have important lessons for us. Let us look at this passage with particular care.

After God brought Israel out of Egypt false prophets rose up from time to time to controvert the truth that He revealed through His specially anointed servants. From the days when Korah, Dathan, and Abiram opposed Moses right on down to the period immediately preceding the captivity of Israel and Judah heretical teachers tried to mislead God's people. God's true servants were opposed by these false prophets who attempted to foist their own dreams upon the people instead of the truth as declared by those who were divinely enlightened. Similar conditions had begun already to prevail in Christian circles even in apostolic times, and God foresaw that false teachers would rise up throughout all the centuries prior to the return of our Lord Jesus Christ.

False teachers come in under cover. They bring in heresies privately or secretly. It is never customary for teachers of error to declare and oppose the truth openly in the beginning. As a rule they work in an underhanded way, seeking to gain the confidence of God's people before they make known their real views. Such false teachers often hide their doctrinal peculiarities by using orthodox terms to which, however, they attach an altogether different meaning than that which is ordinarily accepted. Once having wormed their way into the confidence of the people of God they go to the limit, even denying the Lord who bought them, and so exposing themselves to the judgment of God. If they alone were judged by God it would be comparatively a small thing, but the sad result of their unscriptural ministry is that the weak and uninstructed readily follow them. And because of this the way of truth—that is, "the faith which was once delivered unto the saints" (Jude 3)—is derided and maligned.

There are many examples today in various circles where the greatest and most precious things of God are spurned and held up to ridicule by those who have believed false views through listening to these heretical teachers. Heresy is like leaven. As the apostle

Paul told us when combating Jewish legality that was spreading among the Galatians, "A little leaven leaveneth the whole lump" (Galatians 5:9). Leaven is corruption, and its nature is to corrupt all with which it comes in contact. So it is with false doctrine.

Behind every system of error is the sin of covetousness. Men seek to draw away disciples after themselves in order that they might profit through them, and so as Peter explained, "Through covetousness shall they with feigned words make merchandise of you" (2:3). If it were not for the money question one wonders how long many systems of error would survive. Alas, that any should be so sordid as to seek to enrich themselves through the credulity of the souls whom they lead astray. Their judgment awaits them like a Damocles sword hanging over their heads, and though it seems to slumber for the moment it will not be long before it falls with terrible effect on all such blind leaders of the blind.

In verse 4 we are referred to the apostasy of some of the angels. These who were created innocent, followed the lead of Satan and sinned even in Heaven. God has not spared them, though they were beings of so high an order; but He cast them down to Tartarus, which is the lowest depth of Hell. There they are held in chains of darkness, awaiting the final judgment. It seems very clear that Scripture contemplates two distinct angelic apostasies. While Satan is the leader in both, they did not occur at the same time. Satan himself is not yet bound in Tartarus, nor will he be until he is cast into the bottomless pit, which is prior to the millennial reign of our Lord Jesus Christ, as we learn from Revelation 20:1-3. The angels that followed him in his first rebellion seem to be identical with the demons who have ever been the opponents of the truth of God and who were specially active in opposition to the Lord Jesus Christ when He was here on earth. Satan is called the prince of the power of the air, and he and his cohorts are still at large and are described as wicked spirits in the heavenlies (Ephesians 2:2). They are thus able to carry on constant warfare against the saints. The sin of the angels mentioned in 2 Peter 2:4, and also in the Epistle of Jude, seems to be of a special character and may be that which is referred to in Genesis 6: 2: "The sons of God saw the daughters of men that they were fair; and they took them wives of all which they chose."

This is admittedly a very mysterious passage, but many have understood it to mean that certain angelic beings, such as are referred to in the book of Job as "sons of God," left their own habitation and came down to earth. They took possession of the bodies of men, stirring them up to unlawful lusts, which resulted in that corruption and violence that brought about the deluge.

When that flood spread over all the world, destroying those who persisted in their opposition to the truth, God saved Noah and his family—eight persons in all (2:5). Noah is spoken of here as a preacher of righteousness. He preached, doubtless, not only by word of mouth but also by his actions. It has been well said that every spike that Noah drove into the ark was a sermon to that ungodly generation, declaring that judgment was about to fall.

Next we have reference to the judgment of Sodom and Gomorrha (6). These cities gave themselves over to such vileness that God could no longer tolerate their inhabitants, and so He destroyed them with fire from heaven, making them an example or a warning to those who should in after days live in the same ungodly manner. When God demolished these cities of the plains He delivered righteous Lot, who had lived in Sodom for years though distressed by the filthy behavior of the wicked. We might never have thought of Lot as deserving to be called a righteous man, but the Holy Spirit so speaks of him here. He was a righteous man living in a wrong place. As a result he was in a constant state of vexation; his righteous soul was disturbed continually by what he heard and saw among the people with whom he lived. It is noticeable that though he is here designated as "just" and "righteous" we do not find his name in the eleventh chapter of the Epistle to the Hebrews. It never could have been said that "by faith Lot dwelt in Sodom": it was rather lack of faith that took him there. He hoped that living in the plains of Sodom would better his worldly circumstances. Finally, when the judgment fell he was saved out of it all but "so as by fire" (1 Corinthians 3:14-15). The conflagration destroyed everything for which he had labored during all those years that he had lived in Sodom.

Even as the Lord delivered Noah and Lot before the judgments fell, so now He never forgets His own. He knows how to deliver the godly out of trials, temptations, persecutions, and tribulations of every kind, and to reserve the unjust until the day of judgment to be punished. Often it seems as though the more wicked men are, the more they prosper in this world; whereas the righteous suffer almost continuously. God permits trial to come to His own for their discipline. However He allows the ungodly to have their fling now, as we say, but they will be judged according to their deeds when at last they appear before Him.

Characteristics of Apostate Teachers (2 Peter 2:10-17)

In 2 Peter 2:10 we have certain characteristics brought before us that distinguish false teachers. As there is no power to control their fleshly desires in the untruths they proclaim, they secretly and often openly live in the lust of uncleanness, making excuses for their evil behavior. They despise authority and do not desire to be subject to anyone. They are presumptuous, attempting to explore mysteries that even the most godly dare not look into; they are self-willed, determined to have their own way, and are not afraid to speak evil of those of highest rank, so lifted up are they in their own pride and conceit.

In verses 11-17 we have further evidence of the true nature of these apostates. While these ungodly men vaunt themselves against all authority—human, angelic, or divine—the elect angels do not presume to bring railing accusations even against those of their own order who have apostatized from God. The angels who have been preserved by God from falling into sin, and are greater far in power and might than men here on the earth do not dare to slander the fallen angels. Jude wrote that Michael the archangel did not bring against Satan a railing accusation but simply said, "The Lord rebuke thee" (Jude 9). But these apostate leaders behave like natural brute beasts who are made to be taken and destroyed. These brutes, not possessing intelligence, act in accordance with their own vicious appetites and are imitated by the false teachers. Peter warned against these teachers who oppose truths that God has revealed in His Word but which they do not understand. In refusing the truth they, of necessity, will be left to perish and in due time will be rewarded according to the unrighteousness of their lives. They have lived as though their greatest object was to satisfy the desires of their own hearts. They have counted it a pleasure to riot in the daytime: the night will find them utterly unprepared for the judgment they have so richly deserved.

As these teachers of error mingle among the people of God they are spots and blemishes, marring and disturbing the fellowship of the saints, giving themselves over to self-indulgence as they feast with Christians as though they belonged to the family of God. Because there is no power in error to subdue nature's sinful lusts they are described as having "eyes full of adultery"; they cannot cease from sin. It is only the might of the Holy Spirit that can subdue and control the lusts of the flesh. False doctrines never do this. While deceiving or leading astray "unstable souls"—that is, those who are not well-grounded in the truth of God—they prove themselves to be an accursed generation. Their hearts are exercised not unto godliness but with covetous practices.

Verse 15 tells us that having renounced the right way they have gone astray, following the way of Balaam, the son of Bosor (Beor), who loved the wages of unrighteousness. While pretending to be subject to the Lord, Balaam craved the riches that Balak offered him if he could curse Israel for him (Numbers 22). As Balaam hurried on his way, lured by the desire of gain, even the beast on which he rode rebuked him, as it beheld an angel of God in the way who tried to turn back the covetous prophet from his path. Men may ridicule and sneer at the idea of an ass speaking with a man's voice, but he who knows the Lord will remember that with God all things are possible.

While the propagators of unholy and unscriptural theories profess to have just the message that men need, they actually have nothing that can give victory over sin or relief to a troubled conscience. They are like wells without water that only disappoint the thirsty who go to them. These false teachers are also like clouds that look as though they might soon pour down refreshing showers but are carried away by gales of wind, and so the land is left as dry and arid as ever. The doom of these misleading teachers is sure: blackest darkness is to be their portion forever. The sad thing is that even among professing Christians so many are ready to listen to these pretentious vendors of false systems. Finally they are disappointed and fall when they find that they are left without anything on which the heart and conscience can rest for eternity.

Forsaking the Truth to Follow False Philosophies (2 Peter 2:18-22)

It is one thing to accept Christianity as a system; it is quite another to know Christ as Savior and Lord. All who are truly born again can say, "greater is he that is in [me], than he that is in the world" (1 John 4:4). True children of God are kept from error as they live in dependence on His Word as it is opened up to them by the Holy Spirit. But those who have merely accepted a system of doctrines, however sound, are always in danger of giving them up for some other system and so becoming apostates. They are ensnared by the boastful language of false teachers who allure through the lusts of the flesh by presenting doctrines that appeal to careless hearts. Those who at one time had seemingly been completely delivered from sin and its folly are easily misled into thinking that they are learning something superior to that which they already possess. But while these teachers promise their victims liberty they themselves are slaves of corruption, because they know nothing of the liberty of grace. Accustomed to undisciplined freedom they are easily overcome by sin and brought into bondage.

Verses 20 and 21 have been understood by some as teaching that after people have been truly born again they are in danger of ceasing to be children of God and becoming once more the seed of Satan. It is well to observe that the Spirit of God is not contemplating the one who has made a sincere profession. Rather He speaks of those who "have escaped the pollutions of the world through the knowledge of the Lord and Saviour Jesus Christ"; that is, having accepted the doctrines of Christianity they have professed to give up the world, its sins, and its folly but there has never been a new nature imparted. They have not been born of God. Consequently, they always have the desire to gratify the lusts of the flesh, and when they come in contact with these false teachings they are easily entangled and overcome, and so their latter end is worse than the beginning. Having given up the profession of Christianity and adopted some false and unholy system of teaching they throw off all restraint as to their lusts and live even more vilely than they did before they made a profession of conversion. Of these Peter said, "It had been better for them not to have known the way of righteousness, than, after they have known it, to turn from the holy commandment delivered unto them" (21).

Anyone who becomes acquainted with the teachings of Christianity knows the way of righteousness. Men may give adherence to that way for the time being but not actually know Christ for themselves. Of those who have thus apostatized we read, "It is happened unto them according to the true proverb, The dog is turned to his own vomit again; and the sow that was washed to her wallowing in the mire" (22). Charles H. Spurgeon well said on one occasion, "If that dog or that sow had been born again and had received the nature of a sheep it never would have gone back to the filth here depicted." The dog is used as a symbol of false teachers on more than one occasion in Scripture. The sow is the natural man who may be cleansed outwardly but still loves the hog-wallow, and as soon as restraint is off he will go back to the filth in which he once lived.

CHAPTER THREE

LOOKING TO THE FUTURE

As Peter looked forward to the day when he would seal his own testimony for Christ by laying down his life, as the Lord had foretold, he was anxious to remind the saints of the importance of maintaining their confidence in God's revelation concerning the last days. He had already reminded those to whom he wrote that prophecy is a lamp to lighten the pilgrim along the dark road as he pursues his way through this world to the Canaan rest awaiting him (2 Peter 1:19).

In 2 Peter 3 he stressed the importance of keeping the testimony of the prophets and apostles in mind, when many will spurn them entirely.

Dangers of Forgetting the Past and Denying the Future (2 Peter 3:1-7)

In writing this second letter, guided by the Spirit of God, Peter was not endeavoring so much to open up new vistas of truth as to encourage the saints to keep in memory what they had learned already. The words that were spoken in Old Testament times by the holy prophets, and the additional revelations communicated through the apostles of the new dispensation, should never be forgotten. Peter himself wrote as one of the latter group, having been definitely commissioned as an apostle by the Lord Jesus, and recognized by his brethren as being peculiarly adapted to make known the gospel to the Jews. Paul wrote in the Epistle to the Galatians that the brethren at Jerusalem acknowledged that the gospel of the uncircumcision had been committed to him and the gospel of the circumcision had been committed to Peter (Galatians 2:7). This is not to suppose that he meant by this statement that there was any fundamental difference in the messages themselves. It was rather that God had fitted Paul in a very definite way to carry the gospel to the Gentiles; whereas Peter was more adapted to minister the Word of grace to the Jews. As a result of Peter's ministry many of the dispersion had been brought to know the Lord. And in obedience to the command given Peter on the shore of the sea of Galilee he undertook to feed these sheep and lambs of Christ's flock both by word of mouth and in these Epistles.

He admonished them therefore in the strongest possible way regarding the necessity of keeping in mind the Holy Scriptures of the Old and New Testaments. The Old Testament had been complete for centuries, but the New Testament was not yet complete. Nevertheless many of its books were in circulation already, and among them were all the Epistles of Paul, as we shall see later in considering the closing verses of this chapter. Peter recognized in these books the testimony of God Himself who, by the Holy Spirit, had inspired the human authorship of each portion of the Word. He urged the saints not to neglect the Scriptures but keep them in their hearts, in order that they may shed light on both their present and future pathway.

It had been predicted again and again by both prophets and apostles that in the last days there would be those who would utterly repudiate the truth of a divine revelation concerning the return of the Lord. These scoffers would hate the truth because it interfered with their own selfish desires, and would sneer at the very possibility of the second advent of the Savior. Peter spoke of these scoffers as being in the future and "in the last days" and we now see them all around us. Everywhere we find men following their own ungodly lusts, deriding the doctrine of the imminent return of the Lord as though it were something utterly ridiculous and not to be considered for a moment by sensible people. Even in the pulpits of professedly orthodox churches there are many ministers today who take this stand. They either deny that the Bible itself teaches the second coming of Christ, or else maintain that even though

predicted by Christ and taught by His apostles, it is all to be looked
upon as an idle dream. These men ask contemptuously, "Where is
the promise of his coming?" They declare that "since the fathers
fell asleep, all things continue as they were from the beginning of
the creation" (4). In other words, they insist that there is no evidence whatever in the history of the past or in conditions prevailing
at the present time that indicate the fulfillment of any prophetic
declarations. Though wise in the things of this world, they are absolutely ignorant of the signs of the times—signs readily discerned by
spiritually-minded and godly men, but ignored completely by carnal and sensual leaders of religious thought. As in the days before
the flood the men of Noah's day refused to believe the warning of
an impending judgment and knew not until the flood came and took
them all away, so will it be with many in this generation who contemptuously discard all that Scripture teaches in regard to the coming day of the Lord (see Matthew 24:37-39). Yet the world is rushing steadily forward into the fearful vortex of that day of wrath.

Many have forgotten that "by the word of God the heavens were
of old, and the earth standing out of the water and in the water:
Whereby the world that then was, being overflowed with water,
perished" (2 Peter 3:5-6). The men who lived in antediluvian times
said to God, "Depart from us; for we desire not the knowledge of
thy ways" (Job 21:14). As Eliphaz reminded Job when he said:

> Hast thou marked the old way which wicked men have trodden?
> Which were cut down out of time, whose foundation was
> overflown with a flood: Which said unto God, Depart from us:
> and what can the Almighty do for them? Yet he filled their
> houses with good things: but the counsel of the wicked is far
> from me (Job 22:15-18).

So it will be with many in this age. They are willingly ignorant
of God's dealings with men in the past, and therefore refuse to believe any predictions of judgments to come.

There is something very striking in the expression, "kept in store,
reserved unto fire" (3:7). The passage might be translated "the heavens and the earth are stored with fire, awaiting the day of judgment

and perdition of ungodly men." We might have some conception of what this means as we think of the fearful catastrophe produced by the atomic bomb, which was, even to those who created it, a terrible revelation of the powers for destruction. When earth's long day has run its course there will come not another flood but a universal conflagration that will sweep this globe clean of all that men have built up during the millennia of the past, and prepare for a new heaven and a new earth wherein dwelleth righteousness.

The Day of the Lord and the Day of God (2 Peter 3:8-14)

Because willfully ignorant men do not see the evidences of the Lord's return they deny what they do not understand. As the writer of Ecclesiastes said, "Because sentence against an evil work is not executed speedily, therefore the heart of the sons of men is fully set in them to do evil" (8:11). If judgment seems to tarry it is not that God has forgotten, but rather because of His deep concern for lost men whom, in His lovingkindness, He still desires to save. Our thoughts are not His thoughts, neither are our ways His ways, but as the heavens are higher than the earth, so are His ways above our ways, and His thoughts above our thoughts (see Isaiah 55:8-9). A thousand years may seem a long time to men whose span of life very seldom reaches a century, but one day is with the Lord as a thousand years, and a thousand years as one day. Not two days have passed, therefore, according to the divine reckoning, since the Lord Jesus went away after giving the promise, "I will come again" (John 14:3). It is not that the Lord is slack regarding His promise, as men are disposed to think, but His heart still goes out to those who are persisting in rebellion against Him. He waits in grace, proclaiming the gospel message and offering salvation to all who turn to Him in repentance, because He is not willing that any should perish.

But when at last the day of grace is ended, the day of the Lord will succeed it and that day will come to unbelievers as a thief in the night. The day of the Lord is not to be confused with the day of Christ, which refers to the return of the Lord in the air to call His saints to be with Himself. At that time they will appear before His judgment seat to be rewarded according to the measure of their faithfulness to Him while they have been pilgrims here below. The day of the Lord follows that. It will be the time when the judgments of God are being poured out upon the earth. It includes the descent of the Lord with all His saints to execute judgment on His foes, and to take possession of the kingdom so long predicted, and to reign in righteousness for a thousand glorious years in this very world where He once was crucified.

As that great day of the Lord closes, the heavens and the earth "shall pass away with a great noise, and the elements shall melt with fervent heat" (3:10). This last expression is far easier understood today than it ever has been in past centuries because of discoveries in connection with the explosive power of certain elements such as uranium when brought under terrific pressure. Following the destruction of the created heavens and this lower universe as we now know them, will come the fulfillment of the prediction of Isaiah 65:17 concerning a new heaven and a new earth wherein righteousness will dwell forever. This eternal condition is the day of God, in view of which the present created heavens and earth will be destroyed. The day of God is unending; it includes all the ages to come when sin will be forever banished from the universe, and righteousness will be displayed everywhere. Righteousness suffers during the present age. Those who live in obedience to the Word of God often are persecuted by those who seek to maintain the present order of things. In the millennium righteousness will reign: the authority of the Lord Jesus will be everywhere established, and evil will be held down. But in the eternal state righteousness will dwell, for all evil will have been banished to the lake of fire.

A Final Warning (2 Peter 3:15-18)

God's patience and longsuffering with mankind throughout all the centuries of human history are ever with a view to the salvation of any who will turn to Him, confessing their sin and believing the message of His grace.

Peter added, "Even as our beloved brother Paul also according to the wisdom given unto him hath written unto you" (15). This is very clearly an authentication of the Pauline authorship of the Epistle to the Hebrews. There can be no other writing to which he referred in this verse. As we have seen, Peter himself addressed converted Jews or Hebrews. He told us that the apostle Paul had written a letter to the same people. There is no other of Paul's letters addressed to converted Jews but the Epistle to the Hebrews. The testimony of Peter in this Epistle concerning eschatological truths corroborated Paul's message. In Hebrews 12:25-29 we read:

> See that ye refuse not him that speaketh. For if they escaped not who refused him that spake on earth, much more shall not we escape, if we turn away from him that speaketh from heaven: Whose voice then shook the earth: but now he hath promised, saying, Yet once more I shake not the earth only, but also heaven. And this word, Yet once more, signifieth the removing of those things that are shaken, as of things that are made, that those things which cannot be shaken may remain. Wherefore we receiving a kingdom which cannot be moved, let us have grace, whereby we may serve God acceptably with reverence and godly fear: For our God is a consuming fire.

Here we have set forth exactly the same truths that the apostle Peter emphasized in his second Epistle. There should be no question therefore but that Peter was declaring that Paul was the author of the Epistle to the Hebrews.

Then Peter went on to say that in Paul's letter to the Hebrews, as also in all his Epistles, there are "some things hard to be understood, which they that are unlearned and unstable wrest, as they do also the other scriptures, unto their own destruction" (2 Peter 3:16). In this way Peter acknowledged Paul's letters to be accepted by all believers as the very Word of God. There are, in the Epistle to the Hebrews particularly, a number of passages that have caused much distress to those who have but a feeble understanding of God's great plan. Take such passages, for instance, as Hebrews 6:4-8 and 10:26-31. How often has the devil used these Scriptures to trouble unstable souls with the awful thought that perhaps they have committed some unpardonable sin and so are hopelessly beyond the reach of mercy! While the passages themselves suggest nothing of the kind, yet they have been used of the enemy to disturb many. In others of Paul's writings there are passages that have been misused in the same way, but more notable in Hebrews than in any other Epistle.

Peter closed with two admonitions. In verse 17 he said, "Ye therefore, beloved, seeing ye know these things before, beware lest ye also, being led away with the error of the wicked, fall from your own stedfastness." No one will ever fail who keeps his eyes on Christ and his heart fixed on those things that are above where Christ sits at God's right hand. Doctrinal error of a serious character is almost invariably connected with some moral failure. As we walk before God in holiness of life we will be preserved from destructive heresies, and as we walk in the truth we will be kept from sin.

The final admonition is found in the last verse: "Grow in grace, and in the knowledge of our Lord and Saviour Jesus Christ." This is the unfailing panacea for all spiritual ills. As we go on to know Christ better and become increasingly like Him, and as we feed on His Word, and it controls our hearts, our progress will be consistent and continuous.

The final doxology is a very brief but a very precious one: "To him be glory both now and for ever. Amen." How Peter's own heart must have been moved as he wrote these words! He had known Christ intimately in the days of His flesh; he himself had failed so grievously on the night of the betrayal; he had been restored so blessedly, both secretly and publicly, by the Lord Himself. Christ had become the all-absorbing passion of his soul. He alone deserved all the praise and all the glory, and that to the age of ages—the uttermost limits of that day of God, the day of eternity of which we have been reading.

AUTHOR BIOGRAPHY

HENRY ALLAN IRONSIDE, one of this century's greatest preachers, was born in Toronto, Canada, on October 14, 1876. He lived his life by faith; his needs at crucial moments were met in the most remarkable ways.

Though his classes stopped with grammar school, his fondness for reading and an incredibly retentive memory put learning to use. His scholarship was well recognized in academic circles with Wheaton College awarding an honorary Litt. D. in 1930 and Bob Jones University an honorary D.D. in 1942. Dr. Ironside was also appointed to the boards of numerous Bible institutes, seminaries, and Christian organizations.

"HAI" lived to preach and he did so widely throughout the United States and abroad. E. Schuyler English, in his biography of Ironside, revealed that during 1948, the year HAI was 72, and in spite of failing eyesight, he "gave 569 addresses, besides participating in many other ways." In his eighteen years at Chicago's Moody Memorial Church, his only pastorate, every Sunday but two had at least one profession of faith in Christ.

H. A. Ironside went to be with the Lord on January 15, 1951. Throughout his ministry, he authored expositions on 51 books of the Bible and through the great clarity of his messages led hundreds of thousands, worldwide, to a knowledge of God's Word. His words are as fresh and meaningful today as when first preached.

The official biography of Dr. Ironside, *H. A. Ironside: Ordained of the Lord*, is available from the publisher.

THE WRITTEN MINISTRY OF
H. A. IRONSIDE

Expositions

Joshua
Ezra
Nehemiah
Esther
Psalms (1-41 only)
Proverbs
Song of Solomon
Isaiah
Jeremiah
Lamentations
Ezekiel
Daniel
The Minor Prophets
Matthew
Mark
Luke
John

Acts
Romans
1 & 2 Corinthians
Galatians
Ephesians
Philippians
Colossians
1 & 2 Thessalonians
1 & 2 Timothy
Titus
Philemon
Hebrews
James
1 & 2 Peter
1,2, & 3 John
Jude
Revelation

Doctrinal Works

Baptism
Death and Afterward
Eternal Security of the Believer
Holiness: The False and
   the True
The Holy Trinity

Letters to a Roman Catholic
   Priest
The Levitical Offerings
Not Wrath But Rapture
Wrongly Dividing the Word
   of Truth

Historical Works

The Four Hundred Silent Years
A Historical Sketch of the Brethren Movement

Other works by the author are brought back into print from time to time. All of this material is available from your local Christian bookstore or from the publisher.

LOIZEAUX

A Heritage of Ministry . . .

Paul and Timothy Loizeaux began their printing and publishing activities in the farming community of Vinton, Iowa, in 1876. Their tools were rudimentary: a hand press, several fonts of loose type, ink, and a small supply of paper. There was certainly no dream of a thriving commercial enterprise. It was merely the means of supplying the literature needs for their own ministries, with the hope that the Lord would grant a wider circulation. It wasn't a business; it was a ministry.

Our Foundation Is the Word of God

We stand without embarrassment on the great fundamentals of the faith: the inspiration and authority of Scripture, the deity and spotless humanity of our Lord Jesus Christ, His atoning sacrifice and resurrection, the indwelling of the Holy Spirit, the unity of the church, the second coming of the Lord, and the eternal destinies of the saved and lost.

Our Mission Is to Help People Understand God's Word

We are not in the entertainment business. We only publish books and computer software we believe will be of genuine help to God's people, both through the faithful exposition of Scripture and practical application of its principles to contemporary need.

Faithfulness to the Word and consistency in what we publish have been hallmarks of Loizeaux through four generations. And that means when you see the name Loizeaux on the outside, you can trust what is on the inside. That is our promise to the Lord...and to you.

If Paul and Timothy were to visit us today they would still recognize the work they began in 1876. Because some very important things haven't changed at all...this is still a ministry.